HOCKEY'S POWERBROKERS

Art Direction: Leanne Gilbert
Cover Design: Leanne Gilbert
Graphic Design: François Daxhlet, Colin Elliott
Photo Research: Colin Elliott
Project Editor: Ronnie Shuker
Fact-checkers: Malcolm Campbell
Copy Editor: Rachel Villari
Proofreader: Luke Sawczak

Cover information
Clockwise from top left: Dave Reginek/NHLI via
Getty Images, Lucas Oleniuk/Toronto Star via Getty
Images, Steve Babineau/NHLI via Getty Images, Patrick
McDermott/NHLI via Getty Images, Rocky Widner/
Getty Images and Joe Sargent/NHLI via Getty Images.

EXCLUSIVE DISTRIBUTOR :

For Canada and the United States:
Simon & Schuster Canada
166 King Street East, Suite 300
Toronto, ON M5A 1J3
phone: (647) 427-8882
           1-800-387-0446
Fax: (647) 430-9446
simonandschuster.ca

Catalogue data available from Bibliothèque et Archives
nationales du Québec

09-17

© 2017, Juniper Publishing,
division of the Sogides Group Inc.,
a subsidiary of Québecor Média Inc.
(Montreal, Quebec)

Legal deposit: 2017
National Library of Québec
National Library of Canada

ISBN 978-1-988002-65-1

Conseil des Arts   Canada Council
du Canada   for the Arts

We gratefully acknowledge the support of the Canada
Council for the Arts for its publishing program.

We acknowledge the financial support of the
Government of Canada through the Canada Book Fund
for our publishing activities.

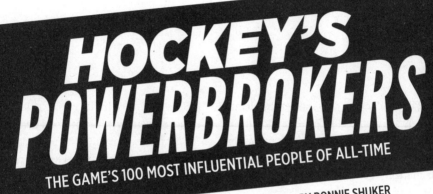

HOCKEY'S POWERBROKERS

THE GAME'S 100 MOST INFLUENTIAL PEOPLE OF ALL-TIME

EDITED BY RONNIE SHUKER

The Hockey News

INTRODUCTION

IN THE UNLIKELY event that you get the chance to celebrate your 100th birthday, go ahead and give yourself a gold star. Bask in the glory, accept every piece of praise fawned upon you and feel free to tell all those 90-year-old whippersnappers to eat your shorts.

That's because getting there is no easy feat, even if you live in the United States or Canada. In the 2010 U.S. census, out of a population of 309 million, only 53,364 Americans were 100 years or older. In Canada's 2011 census, just 5,825 of 33.5 million Canadians were centenarians. In both cases, that's less than 0.02 percent of the population.

Reaching 100 is so difficult that even inorganic persons have trouble getting to the hallowed mark.

According to American and Canadian law, corporations are "persons," too. Perhaps surprisingly, though, these paper people have almost as much difficulty reaching 100 years old as us humans do. In 2011, *USA Today* reported that only 486 publicly traded companies and just 23 private firms in the United States are 100 years or older.

So yeah, this living until 100 thing – it's rare, even if you're not a real person.

That makes the NHL's 100th birthday something worth celebrating. With a nice round three-digit number to work with, *The Hockey News* has honored the league's centennial season by picking out the game's greatest powerbrokers, both on and off the ice, throughout hockey history. We've been doing a smaller version of this for the better part of two decades since we published our first People of Power & Influence magazine on Dec. 31, 1999. Our annual list includes people, *real* people, from across the hockey world – players, coaches, general managers, executives, owners, reporters and even bloggers.

Hockey's Powerbrokers takes this a step further. Using the NHL's centennial as an Archimedean point, we've surveyed all of hockey history and picked out the 100 most powerful and influential people ever. All of the people on the list contributed to the NHL's impressive longevity in one way or another – some, like Lord Stanley (No. 29) and James Creighton (No. 40), before the league was born, while others, like Sidney Crosby and Alex Ovechkin, are still leaving their mark on the game.

The annual magazine list is determined internally. For *Hockey's Powerbrokers*, however, we borrowed the brains of 10 of the brightest hockey minds, including one of our own (sorry, no centenarians) to come up with our all-time list:

- Alan Adams, hockey writer
- Ken Campbell, senior writer at *The Hockey News*
- Steve Dryden, senior managing editor, Hockey Content at TSN
- Bob Duff, sports columnist at the *Windsor Star*
- Helene Elliott, sports columnist at the *Los Angeles Times*
- Kerry Fraser, former NHL referee, columnist at TSN
- Stu Hackel, former NHL director of broadcasting, former *NY Times* and SI.com hockey columnist.
- Pierre McGuire, hockey analyst at NBC
- Paul Patskou, hockey historian
- Szymon Szemberg, managing director at the Alliance of European Hockey Clubs

The criterion was simple: choose the 100 people that have had the biggest impact, *positively or negatively*, on the game of hockey. We collected our panellists' picks, weighed them equally through an inverse points system (1st-place vote = 100 points, 2nd = 99, 3rd = 98 and so on, all the way down to 100 = 1 point) and then tallied the points for all 10 lists. The result is the definitive ranking of hockey's all-time movers and shakers.

As with any list, heated discussion ensued once we compiled the final list. And that's the whole point. *Hockey's Powerbrokers* doesn't close the conversation. It's meant to open it. So let the great debate begin, starting with No. 1 on our list – none other than The Great One himself, Wayne Gretzky.

– By Ronnie Shuker

TABLE OF CONTENTS

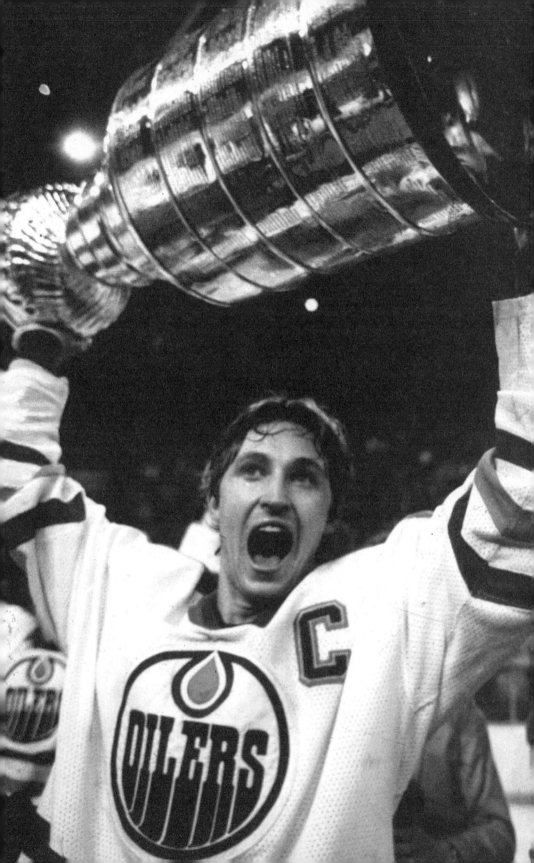

1 WAYNE GRETZKY

AS A TEENAGER playing against men, he was called 'The Kid.' But the nickname that stuck came from the mid-1970s film *The Great Gatsby*, based on F. Scott Fitzgerald's 1925 novel. He was 'The Great Gretzky,' and that has long since been shortened to The Great One.

Wayne Gretzky's otherworldly scoring exploits were indeed great and brought him international attention before he was even a teenager. How he handled all the attention – with modesty, grace and poise – was equally great, and what he contributed to the sport remains immeasurable.

It's doubtful anyone else has affected hockey in such a wide array of areas. Gretzky's influence has been felt everywhere. He changed hockey on the ice, off the ice and in places where it was barely visible.

As he rewrote the record book, Gretzky was also revolutionizing offensive hockey when he entered the NHL with Edmonton in 1979 following a stunning pro debut season in the WHA. He blended features of European hockey with the North American style to usher in an era in which opponents had to stop plays, not players.

He was "the first of our great scorers who essentially plays with the other four skaters," Ken Dryden told *Sport Magazine*'s David Levine in May 1984, the eve of the first of four Oilers Stanley Cups, when that U.S. monthly put Gretzky on the cover, proclaiming "Admit It, America – Wayne Gretzky is the Best Player in *Any* Sport" and publishing three articles' worth of evidence. "The Hulls, the Espositos,

the Mahovlichs were the driving force of their units, and the others were support players to them, and in many ways put with them for that purpose," Dryden said. But Gretzky was different. His games resembled movies in which he starred in the lead role, his teammates became supporting actors and players on other teams were left as the extras you only notice in the credits. "Gretzky gives up the puck to someone in better position, to move in turn into a better position to get the puck back," Dryden continued. "It creates all sorts of interesting and ambitious schemes which all function as a distraction."

The scoring chances he produced came from unusual places – not just the wings or in front of the net, but behind the net as well. "He went to areas where there was nobody," said Scotty Bowman. "The puck would come to him, and now he's got time and space. He was also one of the first to hang up high. He didn't come back in his own end. He lurked on the off-wing side up high. Then he'd take the puck inside, curl and find those late guys."

As many have noted, Gretzky's genius was rooted in his ability to anticipate where the puck was going to go. He also possessed an incredible awareness of everyone else on the ice. "He was fearless for his size," added Bowman, who recalled thinking Gretzky was "almost frail" when he watched him as a junior. "But he kept chugging along."

Off the ice, that relatively small frame and those relatively delicate facial features –

unlike the stereotypical hulking, scarred image of a skater from the 1970s – may have been the keys to Gretzky's unprecedented popularity. He not only played differently, he looked different, like the boy next door – a boy who would regularly defy the odds and the critics on his road to glory.

Sport Magazine's John Capouya wrote a phrase in his 1984 Gretzky profile that was frequently quoted for years afterward – that Gretzky's influence "transcends hockey." We tend to examine that influence now in connection with his move to Los Angeles, which opened up new vistas for the game and enlarged the hockey map, but he first conquered his homeland. "Wayne had a tremendous impact in Canada, which might be taken for granted today," said Puck Agency president Jay Grossman, who has represented numerous NHL players for more than three decades.

In 1984, Capouya spoke with Canadian national radio personality Peter Gzowski, who had interviewed Gretzky on national radio 10 years earlier, when the phenom was just 13, and then written a book on The Great One's young and rising Oilers team. Gzowski called Gretzky "the greatest phenomenon this country has ever seen." Capouya reported that Gretzky's endorsements in 1984 (soft drinks, apparel, cereal, insurance and toys) earned "four to five times his hockey salary" and pointed out that even "his haircuts have national repercussions."

Four years later, when Gretzky married Janet Jones, Canadians treated the event like a royal wedding. Only a few weeks later, when he was traded to Los Angeles, they considered it a national disaster.

Not so the Kings, the NHL or Gretzky himself, though. With the game's biggest star in a city of stars, hockey became front-page news in a huge media market where it had been an afterthought, and echoed it nationwide. "People said, 'I need to be at Kings games,'" said the team's TV voice, Bob Miller. "The first week, they had to put extra people on the phones. They sold something like 5,000 season tickets in a week. We had never seen anything like that."

Celebrities flocked to watch Gretzky and the Kings, generating a new level of national attention for the sport in the U.S. "The locker room after games was like a Hollywood party," Miller recalled. "There were so many stars in there. It was crazy." Post-game team gatherings at the famous West Hollywood celebrity hangout Chasen's turned festive. "Milton Berle, John Candy, Neil Diamond, Mary Hart – so many stars would be there," Miller said. "And Wayne was in the middle of it all."

Gretzky raised hockey's profile to new heights in America. The Kings' box office success fuelled thinking among NHL owners about expanding to other non-traditional Sunbelt markets in the hopes of repeating it, a process that continues today. "Wayne doesn't like to take credit for that," Miller said. "But I think he did (set off that process)."

It's hard to imagine anyone else performing more high-profile promotional work for hockey in the U.S. than Gretzky, and it was a task he performed gladly, even during his stint as coach and part owner of the perpetually troubled Coyotes from 2005 to 2009. "He's always understood who he was and who he is," Grossman said. "He understood that from a young age, and he wore it very well. I don't think anybody's done it better. I don't think anyone was close."

Equally essential was Gretzky's role in improving the economic landscape for his fel-

low players. As the game's first million-dol-lar-a-year player, Gretzky's trade to the Kings ensured he'd continue earning big bucks. His salary eventually hit $3 million annually with L.A. He'd more than doubled that by the time he ended his career with the New York Rangers.

A rising tide lifts all boats, and Grossman points to salary disclosure in the 1990s as the biggest factor in boosting player salaries. Yet even so, he acknowledged that Gretzky's trade to the Kings may well have been the trigger point in the growth of salaries. "Play-ers started to think about the game more

from a business standpoint than they ever had," he said. "You'd have to say there was a reverb effect of Wayne's trade to L.A. on the salaries of other guys in the league."

The bottom line of Gretzky's influence is something anyone can be a witness to. Just ask a casual fan or a non-fan to name the first hockey player that comes to mind and there's a good chance the answer will be Wayne Gretzky. And that's rather remarkable be-cause, as of this writing, Gretzky retired 17 years ago.

– By Stu Hackel

GARY BETTMAN

ON DEC. 11, 1992, the NHL board of governors confirmed that Gary Bettman would replace interim president Gil Stein as head of the league under the new title of commissioner. In the nearly quarter-century since, Bett-man has guided the game to a new era of bil-lion-dollar broadcasting contracts and an on-ice product considerably different from the one he inherited. He has built up a legion of critics, but he's pushed ahead re-lentlessly and evolved into a bulldozer of a businessman, accepting that there would be collateral damage.

If you watch any of Bettman's press confer-ences, you'll recognize he doesn't readily agree with the premise of many journalists' questions. If your perspective doesn't jive with his, he won't concede you're right simply for the sake of pleasantries. That's not why the world's savviest sports lawyers are well compensated.

And Bettman is nothing if not savvy. You don't survive the likes of hawkish own-ers such as Jeremy Jacobs and the late Bill Wirtz for more than 20 years unless you (a) quickly figure out the lay of the land and (b) sculpt it to serve your vision. And that's pre-cisely what Bettman did very early in his ten-ure, via changes to the NHL constitution that consolidated his power.

Since then, even Bettman's harshest critics would admit he's grown the game. He began with 24 teams. Now he governs 31, with the Vegas Golden Knights entering the NHL in 2017-18. He's increased the NHL's footprint in Europe, and he's been open-minded when it comes to cutting-edge technologies, entertain-ment options and changes to the game, such as the shootout and the crackdown on ob-struction.

But do you want to know the real reason Bettman has been the big dog on the ice

block for as long as he has? It's quite simple. In the NHL's first full season under his watch, revenues were pegged at $732 million. That number is now closing in on $4 billion. And it only gets better. The league's mammoth Canadian TV rights holder deal (worth $5.2 billion through 2025-26) with Rogers Sportsnet could put as much as $15 million into each team's coffers every season. To a moneymaker's moneymaker like the Toronto Maple Leafs, that's chump change. But for teams that claim to live or die financially depending on whether they make the playoffs and win a round or two, that's a lifesaver.

And that's one of the hallmarks of the Bettman era. With a few exceptions – the Quebec Nordiques, the original Winnipeg Jets and the Atlanta Thrashers that became the Jets 2.0 – Bettman has managed to keep his house in order. He kept the Coyotes in Arizona when most people had written their

obituary. He brought in a new ownership group for that franchise and a slew of others who were imperiled to various degrees (including the Florida Panthers, St. Louis Blues, Buffalo Sabres and Tampa Bay Lightning). He championed the Canadian assistance plan to help buoy some of the smaller-market northern clubs while the Canadian Dollar was bottoming out. He convinced his employers to help cover the costs of payrolls in New Jersey and Dallas until he found new owners. And he moved the Detroit Red Wings into the Eastern Conference and the Jets into the West.

You don't get everything you want as an owner in his NHL, but in every new collective bargaining agreement, he's got at least one goodie for you. In the most recent labor deal, if you were a small-market team owner, not only did Bettman arrange a 50/50 split of revenue (as he did for all teams), but he further restricted the ability of big-market franchises to bury lucrative contracts in the minor leagues. If you were a big-market team owner, Bettman allowed you to use your largesse by disposing of two unproductive players per team via amnesty buyouts.

What has been productive for Bettman's NHL is the way it has employed advancements in technology to reach fans. Remember, the history of the league includes the career of late Hawks owner Wirtz, who infamously refused to allow his team's home games to be televised. But under Bettman's stewardship, the league appears on the vanguard of social media and has done stellar work promoting its brand on constantly changing platforms. "What we're going to continue to see is the evolution of a fan's ability to connect with the game in ways that previously had been unheard of," Bettman said. "And whether or not it's on TV by cable or satellite, whether it's streamed onto a TV set or a tablet or a computer screen, whether or not it's by mobility, whether or not it's entire games or clips of games or statistics or stories or wraparound programming, we are committed to giving our fans the most complete experience they have to connect them to the game."

Bettman's habit of bitter labor disruptions has interfered with this connection far too regularly. It doesn't matter who has been running the NHLPA – Bob Goodenow in 2004-05 or Donald Fehr in 2012-13 – the tactics of Bettman and legal firm Proskauer Rose Goetz & Mendelsohn have been clear: owners begin negotiations with a lowball process, test the union's mettle by freezing them out and eventually settle. But Bettman is unrepentant of the route he's chosen. Considering the way fans rushed back to embrace the product immediately after the past two lockouts, it's understandable that he should be emboldened by the process. "It's terrible and unfortunate when you can't make a deal without a labor disruption, but it's more important that you have the right economic system," Bettman said. "What we achieved was basically the same revenue-sharing formula between the players and the clubs that had then been put recently in place by both football and basketball. It was something we felt was important. We had hoped we didn't have to go through a work stoppage, but sometimes those things are unavoidable. But the worst of it is obviously the impact it has on the fans and the people who work in the business."

The consensus among hockey people is clear: Bettman is never going to be the most charismatic man in the room, unless it's a one-person room. He's never going to be the most popular man in the room, especially if that room is filled with fans and NHL player agents. But whichever room he's in, Bettman is going to be one of the smarter people, if not the smartest. He's going to be himself, focus on his goals and show not the slightest concern as to what everyone else thinks.

Here's an example. The on-ice Stanley Cup presentation ceremony in which Bettman awards the trophy to the captain of the winning team has become increasingly awkward as fans lustily boo the commissioner. It has been suggested that Bettman step aside and allow a more popular figure to perform the honors. He disagrees. "The fact is, as far as I know, it's always been presented by the president or the commissioner," Bettman said. "That's how it's typically done in other sports. It's a nice tradition. It shows the winning team, the game and the Stanley Cup the appropriate level of respect."

On some level, you have to respect the singularity of purpose one must be consumed by to rationalize that reception and shut out the noise. And if there's something most admirable about the commissioner after 20-plus years, maybe that's it. He knows his job, he knows what his bosses want from him and he has delivered.

Bettman isn't here to paint his face and sit in the stands or hang with players at charity golf tournaments. He's a successful businessman and a human shield for the owners. He came to terms with this long ago.

Maybe the rest of us should, too.

– By Adam Proteau

3 CLARENCE CAMPBELL

IT'S HARD TO cheer for the league commissioner or, in Clarence Campbell's case, the league president. The job is more about business and balancing the books (and the egos of owners) than appealing to fans. And with the passing of time and changing of attitudes, certain behaviors are called into question. Even if it was the right decision on his part to banish Maurice Richard for the end of the 1954-55 season and all of the playoffs for punching a linesman, it's difficult to say whether it was brave, foolish or just plain arrogant of Campbell to show up at the Montreal Forum for the Canadiens' next home game – a move that sparked the infamous Richard Riot.

Campbell grew up in Saskatchewan. He earned a law degree at the University of Alberta and continued his education as a Rhodes Scholar at the University of Oxford. Returning to Edmonton to practise law, Campbell also worked as a referee. From 1936 to 1939, he handled NHL games. During the Second World War, Campbell rose from a private to a lieutenant colonel and later helped prosecute Nazi war criminals.

In 1946, the league offered Campbell the job of assistant to president Red Dutton.

When Dutton resigned soon afterward, Campbell became president on Sept. 4, 1946. He oversaw the extension of the NHL season from 50 to 60 and then 70 games, as well as the creation of the All-Star Game in 1947 to aid player pensions. Campbell guided the NHL through an expansion process, doubling the league's six teams to 12 for the 1967-68 season and tripling them to 18 by 1974-75. He retired in 1977 after a 31-year career, the longest tenure of any North American pro sports leader.

– By Eric Zweig

4 BOBBY ORR

BOBBY ORR IS in a good place. His legacy within the confines of arenas is cemented, he is the best defenseman ever to play the game, and it's difficult to conceive of anyone besting him.

In his second career, success is both present and forthcoming. As president of the Orr Hockey Group player agency, the man who can simply be referred to as 'No. 4' steers the futures of two of the five players to receive exceptional status in the OHL: Aaron Ekblad and Connor McDavid. Ekblad, who was taken first by the Florida Panthers in 2014, won the Calder Trophy after an impressive rookie season. McDavid, on the other hand, went first overall to the Edmonton Oilers in 2015 but had his Calder hopes sidelined by a collarbone injury.

For Orr, it's a reminder of the position he was in 54 years ago as a 14-year-old joining the Oshawa Generals, if not a flashback. There were no endorsements, no panting media for Orr at that time, and major junior hockey didn't even exist. "It was Metro Jr. A then," Orr said. "It was my dream to play in the NHL, and that was the way you had to go. That was the next step. So to be given that opportunity was a thrill."

Thanks to a father who kept things in perspective and didn't let the hype envelop his talented prodigy, Orr spent those early days in the spotlight on an even keel, something he sees in Ekblad and McDavid. But it is nice for the kids to know Orr went through something so few of their peers can relate to. "We talk about it," Orr said. "I'm not a big supporter of

going early (to the OHL). Everybody is in a hurry, and we have to remember it's a marathon, not a sprint. For both of those boys to be players, I didn't really believe they had to go early. They're going to be players. They love being on the ice, they love having a stick in their hand and they have great parents."

Orr's legacy is an intriguing one: eight Norris Trophies for a player forced to retire at 30 due to knee injuries. That's the age when his closest peer in the pantheon, retired Red Wings blueliner Nicklas Lidstrom, started winning the honor of defenseman of the year. How many could Orr have won?

As he detailed in an interview with *The Hockey News* in 1986, Orr tried to "replace hockey with hockey" once it became apparent his playing days were over. He took a job as an assistant with Chicago, the final and only other NHL team he played for, but that lasted just one season.

Scouting was similarly unsatisfying. Perhaps this is why the 1980s view of Orr was that of a bitter soul dwelling on the cruel hand dealt to him. (An article in the now-defunct men's magazine *Quest* by the late Earl McRae was particularly notorious and controversial for taking this stance.) But on more than one occasion back then, Orr made it clear to *THN* that he was doing just fine. He focused on business, moving into condo development, financial printing and marketing and promotional work with Standard Brands, the food conglomerate that merged with Nabisco.

Of course, there were disappointments. Orr had to pull out of the legendary Summit Series because of injury, practising but never playing with the Canadians in their iconic showdown with the Soviets. Modern medicine just wasn't that modern in 1972. Would Orr have gotten into those games based on today's technology? "There's no question," he said. "With today's scopes and the ways they do the surgery, the products out there, for any athlete back a few years, it would be better for them today. When I was playing, you'd ice it, you'd heat it – there was a hot gel – and that was it."

Health and fitness are on Orr's mind these days. Still a man who can move products with his name and influence, he has been touting the LivRelief pain relief cream he and his wife use. But on top of salves, Orr has some advice for those in the world of sports who would still be as cavalier as he was, spurning medical help despite the leaps and bounds made in sports injury treatment. "With to-day's athletes, you're going to get poked," he said. "Get on it right away. There's a lot more you can do today. I thought I'd play forever. When a guy hit me I'd think, 'Oh, it's sore, but I'm going to be all right.' I probably didn't do the things I should have done. The Europeans have forever been so good at preventive medicine. We wait until we hurt and then try to do something about it. Let's try to prevent it. There's a lot we can do to stay in the right condition for sports."

Orr still tries to stay in shape, and he's enthusiastic and energetic whether on his own or in a crowd. He walks, cycles and stretches regularly, his days of lifting weights far behind him. Diet has become a focus, and he relies on his better half to be a partner in that regard. "It's a lot harder now since I don't work out like I used to," he said. "But my wife, Peggy, is a very good cook, and we eat pretty well. We do cheat a bit, but we eat well and I have to. It's much easier putting on the weight now."

Orr has been in the player representative business since the mid-1990s, and the mark he's made off the ice is becoming substantial. His name still adorns one of the teams at the CHL's annual Top Prospects Game, with long-time buddy and former coach Don Cherry taking the other honor.

It's clear that Orr's passion is in the grass-roots. It's been like that for a long time. Not surprising for a kid who began to own the game by playing pond hockey back in Parry Sound, Ont., nor for someone who has seen the best and worst the sport had to offer, from the Stanley Cup to being defrauded by convicted NHL lawyer Alan Eagleson. "It's been a great trip," Orr said. "Parts of it I wish I had been in longer, but the time I had right from my minor hockey days – which are some of my fondest memories – to Oshawa and the Bruins, I was one of the fortunate ones. Parents out there need to keep in mind that .000017 percent of players in hockey play one game in the NHL. Let's not forget why our kids are playing: they're trying to be hockey players. Teach fundamentals, but teach them some values for whatever they do in the future."

At 68, Orr isn't a man in decline or hung up on what might have been. "I can't stand here and say I would have done anything differently," he said. "In a game like hockey, there's a lot of contact, and I played a style where I got hit a lot. I handled the puck a lot and I got hit a lot. That's the game. It was the way I wanted to play, it was the way I enjoyed playing and I'd probably do it all over the same way."

– By Ryan Kennedy

5) SCOTTY BOWMAN ——————

BEFORE SUELLA KNEW her then-boyfriend Scotty Bowman was the man she was going to marry, she waited for him to return from a road trip with the Blues at the airport in St. Louis. His team came back with a tie, and she wasn't quite sure how to react. "She didn't know a lot about hockey, and she told me she wasn't sure if she was supposed to be happy or sad because we had tied," Bowman said. "She decided she should be sad. Right then, I knew she was the one for me."

In retrospect, over the years, there was little cause for Suella to be unhappy.

Bowman coached more games (2,141) and posted more wins (1,244) than any coach in NHL history. Montreal (24), Toronto (13) and Detroit (11) are the only franchises with more Stanley Cups than the nine Bowman won as a coach. More than wins and Cups, however, Bowman will be remembered for his ability to adjust to changing times, to motivate and get the best out of his players and to continue to do so for more than four decades.

The most successful coach in NHL history operated with one philosophy in mind – that neither he nor anyone around him should be taking up residence in the comfort zone. According to Bowman, contentment breeds complacency. "A coach's job is to get the best out of his best players," he said. "Every player is different. What makes

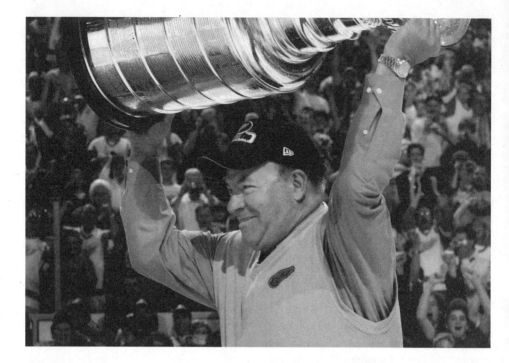

one player tick might make another player ticked off."

Bowman's office was always just inside the door of the dressing room. Everyone was required to pass by, and Bowman might give an unsuspecting player the NHL third degree. Who played last night? What were the scores? Who got the goals? How many points do we have? When's our next game? "Believe me, you'd better have known the answers," said Bob Plager, a defenseman for Bowman's Blues.

As a bench strategist, Bowman was unmatched. "After the game, you were exhausted," said Ken Hitchcock, recalling the games he coached against Bowman. "You were trying to match lines and match wits with Scotty, but just when you thought you'd figured out what he was doing, he'd throw another wrench at you and you'd have to start all over again."

Bowman's refusal to stop learning made him a long-running success. He never be-lieved he'd figured it all out, that there weren't other avenues that could give him an edge. "He wasn't afraid to experiment, to try new innovations," said former Detroit defenseman Larry Murphy.

When the NHL embraced the trap in the mid-1990s, Bowman countered with skill, throwing a five-man unit of former Soviet stars together.

After he won his record ninth Cup as a coach in 2002 and decided to call it a career, those he'd vanquished simply tipped their caps to the man who'd conquered them all, time and again. Among them was Paul Maurice, who as coach of the Carolina Hurricanes lost to Bowman's Red Wings in the 2002 Stanley Cup final. "There are very few times in sports," Maurice said, "that you can watch something unfold and say, 'We're never going to see that happen again.' "

– By Bob Duff

TED LINDSAY

THERE WAS A time when Ted Lindsay wasn't sure he liked his nicknames. Some called him 'Scarface,' others 'Terrible Ted.' "It was these idiots from Toronto, those newspaper writers," Lindsay said.

Lindsay's face is chiselled with the scars of his many hockey wars, resulting in about 700 stitches and so many broken noses he lost count. "I used to be homely when I was younger," he said. "But I had all this involuntary plastic surgery."

Lindsay approached the game only one way. "I had the idea that I should beat up every player I tangled with," he said. "And nothing ever convinced me it wasn't a good idea."

Lindsay made no friends among his NHL opponents. "Ted Lindsay wouldn't even talk to you at the All-Star Game," fellow Hall of Famer Andy Bathgate once said.

Yet the man who was so reviled by other NHLers would be the one who brought them together for their greater good.

In February 1957, the organizing of the NHLPA was announced in New York, with Lindsay as its head. A perennial all-star enjoying an 85-point season with the Detroit Red Wings, one of the faces of the league was now the face of organized labor in hockey. "Don't ask me why I did it," Lindsay said. "I was one of the better hockey players in the world, and I was having one of my best years at the time. But I felt a responsibility, because I saw fellows being sent down. The clubs could send you home – they could send me home – and they didn't owe you five cents. That's not right."

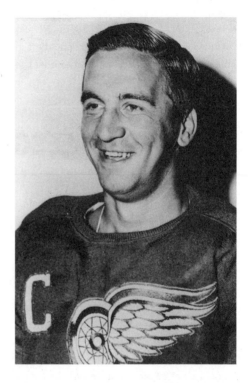

At the time, Lindsay simply stated that the goal of the association was to *promote, foster and protect the best interests of the NHL players*. "We just want to make playing in the league more attractive," Lindsay said. "We're not looking for any trouble."

Just like his time on the ice, though, Lindsay found trouble off it. In July of the same year, even after a stellar campaign, the Wings dealt Lindsay to the lowly Chicago Black Hawks.

The league did agree to some of the NHLPA's conditions during a meeting on Feb. 5, 1958, between NHL governors and representatives for the players, but it refused to recognize the association as an official bargaining unit. It was nearly another decade before the NHLPA officially came to be, but no one in hockey can deny that Lindsay was the man who got the ball rolling.

It was only fitting that in 2010, the NHLPA renamed its player of the year trophy the Ted Lindsay Award. "He was all about doing the right thing," said Hall of Fame defenseman Chris Chelios. "Every player that has played owes him a lot for the sacrifices that he made, what he went through with the Players' Association, the price he paid to make it better for us in the future."

– By Bob Duff

7 ALAN EAGLESON

IN HIS ERA, Alan Eagleson epitomized absolute power, serving as a personification of the old maxim, "Power corrupts and absolute power corrupts absolutely."

The parade of hats that 'The Eagle' donned seemed endless: lawyer, investment counselor, player agent, executive director of the NHLPA, franchise sale broker, chief negotiator for Hockey Canada, promoter, politician and, finally, pariah.

Ken Dryden, Eagleson's goaltender on Canada's 1972 Summit Series squad, called him "a front and center guy." Others were less diplomatic, calling him loud and profane. Eagleson was all that and more.

The conflicts of interest between these jobs eventually became the subject of discord and a long series of articles by Russ Conway for a Massachusetts newspaper beginning in 1991. He reported that Eagleson worked both sides of the labor-management divide to the detriment of the players and his own enrichment, "becoming perhaps the most powerful man in hockey."

The local paper wasn't the only publication to take notice, either. "His power is so immense," *Sports Illustrated* wrote in 1984, "that it makes his position unique in all of sports." In 1989, he was inducted into the Hall of Fame as a builder, the only union leader in sports to be so honored.

Square-jawed and athletically built, Eagleson became hockey's first player agent at a time when most owners and GMs had no tolerance for such an animal. All except, perhaps, the Boston Bruins. When they sought to sign teenage phenom Bobby Orr, he had already pledged his allegiance to Eagleson. The $80,000 two-year deal Eagleson secured for Orr in 1966 more than doubled what established stars Gordie Howe and Bobby Hull earned. Within a few years, his stable included 150 NHL clients.

He parlayed the Orr deal and friendships among the Maple Leafs franchise into organizing and leading the NHLPA, though – likely to ownerships' delight – he wasn't a labor lawyer and had no collective bargaining experience. Hardly a militant, Eagleson's CBA negotiations never proved rancorous to ownership. Still, the players' lot improved markedly, and many became lifelong Eagleson loyalists.

The NHLPA post allowed him to seize a central place in international hockey, beginning with the Summit Series. But as manager of Team Canada, he supported NHL owners' opposition to the breakaway WHA by excluding the rebel league's players, including Bobby Hull, from participating. He continued to organize international events, including Canada Cup tournaments, though he did so not as union head but as a representative of an NHL owner-player partnership.

Storm clouds soon gathered, however. When Orr retired in 1979, the defenseman found he was broke while his agent, who promised to make him a millionaire, was quite wealthy.

Eagleson's rule over the NHLPA became increasingly marked by controversy as questions arose about matters like players' pensions and use of funds. "At NHLPA meetings," *Sports Illustrated* reported, "he would intimidate players who asked questions into silence by snapping curt answers to their queries, embarrassing them in front of their fellows for their ignorance and undermining their dignity."

Few openly opposed him. Those who did, like Boston's Mike Milbury, were outnumbered by Eagleson supporters.

Eventually, the heat generated by player agents from a critical 1989 investigation forced him to announce his resignation in 1992. Meanwhile, Conway (with help from Orr) began exposing corrupt practices and handed information to government investigators in both the United States and Canada. The allegations of skimming insurance payments to injured players were most damning.

Charged with over 30 different crimes in the U.S. in 1994, Eagleson had his prosecution in Canada delayed thanks to his political connections there. His U.S. plea deal resulted in a $700,000 fine. His Canadian guilty plea, including embezzling Canada Cup proceeds, earned an 18-month prison sentence, of which he served six months.

From jail, after numerous honored players threatened they'd quit unless he was removed, Eagleson resigned his membership in the Hall of Fame.

– By Stu Hackel

80 BOB GOODENOW

IF YOU MENTIONED Bob Goodenow's name in NHL circles not long ago, you'd likely have received one of two diametrically opposed reactions: a mixture of grudging respect and out-and-out loathing if you were talking to a team owner, or awe bordering on hero-worship if you were talking to a player or an agent. In the 13 years he ran the NHL Players' Association, Goodenow was one of hockey's most polarizing figures. And the staggering success he enjoyed rebuilding a shattered union eventually became the reason for his ouster in 2005.

The NHLPA was in ruins when Goodenow took the reins in 1992. The union was a victim of Alan Eagleson, its founding executive director who embezzled millions from players and conspired with owners to constrain player wages. Understandably, players sought a replacement who was the polar opposite of Eagleson. They got one in Goodenow, a grim-faced Harvard graduate uninterested in befriending league powerbrokers.

Within weeks of replacing Eagleson, Goodenow orchestrated a show of force and unity by facilitating a 10-day strike on the eve of the 1992 playoffs that ended with substantial NHLPA gains on numerous financial fronts. More importantly, he pushed for and won public salary disclosure for players – a flashlight in a once pitch-dark world where owners concealed the value of their on-ice assets to limit labor costs.

Consequently, NHLers' salaries took off like a drag race without any drag and Goodenow was lauded in every league dressing room and agent's office. This didn't endear him to owners, who, under the leadership of NHL commissioner Gary Bettman, took measures to curtail player costs: the league locked out the NHLPA for 103 days of the 1994-95 season, aiming to implement what Goodenow recognized as a salary cap and was adamant that players not accept. The lockout cost the league 468 games that year, but Goodenow's militant approach led to the owners backing down.

Again, Goodenow's stock within the union soared, and so did his power. Working out of the NHLPA's Toronto office, Goodenow ruled sternly, sourly and autocratically, but he continued pouring money into players' bank accounts and angering owners, some of whom had payrolls as high as $75 million. His ascent to the top of the hockey business world was complete, and he settled in for the next decade. However, the league's determination to achieve cost certainty only strengthened in that timespan, as did the personal loathing some had for Goodenow. And when the NHL locked out players again in 2004-05 and Goodenow reiterated his unwillingness to accept a salary cap, his ouster was on owners' minds. "Owners wanted their cap, but don't think for one minute they didn't also want Bob's head on a platter," said one longtime agent who spoke on condition of anonymity. "Bob wasn't hated by every owner, but you don't win the concessions Bob won without making bitter enemies on the other side. And he just genuinely didn't care. He was working for the players. They're the only ones he cared about. And that made some owners absolutely apoplectic."

But that stubborn determination that had made his reputation as a genius a decade prior proved to be his undoing. Contrary to the outcome of the NHLPA's 1994-95 labor victory, Goodenow underestimated the resolve of Bettman and the owners, who cancelled the entire 2004-05 season rather than play cap-less. In the summer of 2005, Goodenow's constituents mutinied, relented on the cap issue and accepted his resignation shortly after a new collective bargaining agreement was ratified.

For nearly 15 years, Goodenow was one of pro hockey's most important figures. But just as he engineered his own rise through the industry's ranks, he was responsible for the errors that triggered his downfall.

– By Adam Proteau

9 MAURICE RICHARD

MAURICE RICHARD'S NICKNAME was The Rocket, but during his explosive career, which spanned nearly two decades, he was known as the 'Babe Ruth of Hockey.' Quite simply, there is no player, before or since, who has had Richard's dynamic combination of talent and personality. He was the first NHL player to score 50 goals, which he accomplished in 50 games during the 1944-45 season. His 544 career goals were scored with blazing eyes that intimidated netminders. "When Rocket skated in on the net," said Hall of Fame goalie Glenn Hall, "his eyes would shine like a pair of searchlights. It was awesome to see him coming at you."

Richard is the only player in history to have inspired a full-fledged riot. In March 1955, after The Rocket struck a linesman following a fight, NHL president Clarence Campbell announced he had suspended Richard for the final week of the season and the entire playoffs. Protesters destroyed parts of downtown Montreal until Richard went on radio and television to plea for calm. As *Detroit Times* sports columnist Bob Mur- phy opined, "The Rocket was made to watch and write about."

Richard won eight Stanley Cups with Montreal, captaining the Canadiens to the final four of their five consecutive Cups from 1956 to 1960. Scoring in the clutch was The Rocket's forte. His sudden-death overtime goals are legendary, while his leadership and passion were a large part of what made the Canadiens the NHL's most revered dynasty. In a playoff game against the Toronto Maple Leafs on March 23, 1944, he scored three goals in the second period and two more in the third. The final score was remembered as Richard 5, Toronto 1.

Hall of Fame goalie Frank Brimsek put it best: "Richard can shoot from any angle. You play him for a shot to the upper corner and The Rocket wheels around and fires a backhander in the near lower part of the net."

Chicago goalie Emile Francis remembered when Richard scored "with one of my Black Hawks defensemen being carried on his back."

Nobody summed up Richard's influence on the game better than Canadian author Peter Gzowski, though, who concluded, "Richard was the most exciting athlete I had ever seen."

– By Stan Fischler

10 JACQUES PLANTE

NOV. 1, 1959 is a date etched in hockey history. That's when Jacques Plante broke tradition after taking a shot in the face from Andy Bathgate. The puck hit him squarely in the nose, requiring several stitches. He chose to wear a grotesque facemask from that point on.

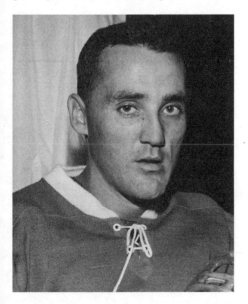

If Plante had done nothing else in his sporting life, the fact he was the first goaltender to introduce a workable facemask into the game would be sufficient for his canonization in the Hall of Fame. But he was much more than that. Plante was a winner and an expert at his profession, as well as creative and durable. He won the Vezina Trophy each year from 1956 through 1960, during which his Montreal Canadiens won five straight Stanley Cups. Plante took another Vezina in 1962 and later shared one with Glenn Hall in 1969, when both tended goal for the St. Louis Blues.

Before Plante entered the NHL, goaltenders rarely left the crease to play the puck. It was Plante who started the trend of stickhandling by going behind the net and passing the rubber to one of his teammates, launching an attack. Eventually, every goalie copied Plante's maneuver, as well as his masks.

– By Stan Fischler

11 FOSTER HEWITT

HE MIGHT NOT have had the classic pipes of many current day broadcasters, but Foster Hewitt did have the unique ability to convey hockey's excitement. The emotion in his voice made live play-by-play essential for hockey fans and provided the foundation other broadcasters built upon. From Hewitt's first hockey game on radio (Feb. 16, 1923) until his final television broadcasts during the 1972 Summit Series, no play-by-play man has ever had as big an impact on the game.

Even before the opening of Maple Leaf Gardens in 1931, Hewitt's broadcasts had gone national. A survey by General Motors (Hewitt's first sponsor) showed that 74 percent of all radios in Canada were tuned to hockey on Saturday nights. For decades, Hewitt was almost as famous as the Leaf greats he covered.

– By Eric Zweig

12 BOBBY HULL

AS AN ALL-STAR left winger for the Chicago Black Hawks, Robert Marvin Hull had it all: supreme talent, charm, charisma, good looks and the know-how to use those qualities to sell the game in the TV age on both sides of the border. Dynamic during play, he was also a great interviewee afterward. And away from the camera, he honored every autograph request, often keeping his team bus waiting.

The third NHLer to break the 50-goal barrier, 'The Golden Jet' scored like few have ever done, and his curly blond hair and radiant smile – even without his two front teeth – became a sports page fixture. He graced the covers of hockey magazines even when they didn't feature a Hull story inside. There was no greater poster boy for hockey during the 1960s.

A speeding Hull in full flight intimidated opponents, and his slapshot terrorized goal-

tenders. That shot became even more troublesome when he and teammate Stan Mikita began curving their stick blades in the mid-1960s, causing the puck to dip and swerve mid-flight. They eventually rendered the straight blade extinct.

Beyond his ability to lift fans from seats as he rushed up the ice, Hull singlehandedly changed hockey's economic landscape. He put money into players' pockets as the league's top-gate attraction. But after regular skirmishes with the Black Hawks over salary, he stunned the NHL by bolting to the new WHA's Winnipeg Jets in 1972 to become the first player to earn a million-dollar deal, catapulting salaries throughout pro hockey while providing instant credibility to the rebel league.

In both the NHL and WHA, Hull railed against hockey's rising violence, even sitting out games in protest. His disdain for goonery only grew after the Jets imported a clutch of highly skilled Swedish stars. They and Hull put a thrilling new brand of hockey on the ice, their elite skills transforming the character of the North American game and inspiring the offensive deluge of the 1980s.

– By Stu Hackel

13 JEAN BELIVEAU

IN ENGLISH THEY called him 'Big Jean.' In French, his nickname was 'Le Gros Bill' (Big Bill). No matter how you'd shake it, Jean Beliveau emerged larger than life as the poster boy for the Montreal Canadiens. His 10 Stanley Cup rings merely underlined the point.

Everything about Beliveau was majestic, from his size – he was the tallest and heaviest of the superstars – to his style, which is best described as looking effortless. "Big Jean had a quiet dignity to go with all his talent," said his one-time teammate Dick Duff. "He was so unassuming for a guy of his stature. He had great moves – that great range. Anybody playing on a line with him was certain to wind up with a lot of goals. If you got there, the puck would be there."

Beliveau didn't get to the NHL right away, though. He didn't need to. As a star playing for the Quebec Aces in the fast and well-paying Quebec Senior League in the early 1950s, he made as much money – if not more. And the adulation came with the dough. When American sportswriter Leonard Shecter visited the Aces' home, he wrote, "When Beliveau walks down the street in Quebec, the women smile, the men shake his hand and the little boys follow him."

The Canadiens brass also followed him, seeking his employment with the NHL club. At first Beliveau resisted. When he finally did sign a big-league contract, however, he set a new precedent by bringing a financial advisor, Emile Couture, with him. Such a practice of being represented by an agent was unheard of in the then-insular NHL.

After signing with Montreal in 1953, Beliveau was challenged to acclimatize himself to The Show. Despite his bulk, Le Gros Bill seemed timid. He was easily pushed around

without giving any pushback. But once Toe Blake took over as coach in 1955, Beliveau became more physically aggressive, and his point totals soared to a level where he was acclaimed alongside Maurice Richard. "The difference between the two best players in the game today," said one critic, "is simply this: Beliveau is a perfectionist while Richard is an opportunist."

Beliveau twice won the Hart Trophy as the NHL's most valuable player and was a first-team all-star in 1955, 1956, 1957, 1959, 1960 and 1961. He was the league's scoring champion in 1956 and won the Conn Smythe Trophy in 1965. He was a pivotal cog in the Montreal scoring machine that won five straight Stanley Cups from 1956 to 1960.

His teammates were delighted to have him in the dressing room, and not only because of his skill. There were always positive vibes emanating from the Beliveau stall. Even rival coaches, such as hard-bitten George 'Punch' Imlach of the Toronto Maple Leafs, admired him. "It's practically impossible for anyone who knows Bill well to have any ill feelings toward Jean," Imlach said. "He would go on the ice, play one heckuva game, change and leave without saying much. He was one player all the fellows liked."

That sweet feeling lingered into the 1971 playoffs, when he scored one of the most spectacular goals of his career, powering his underdog Habs past Bobby Orr's heavily favored Boston Bruins in the first round. Beliveau retired after winning the final Cup of his career. As always, his timing was exquisite.

– By Stan Fischler

14 GORDIE HOWE

THE NICKNAME SAYS it all: Mr. Hockey. He is not 'The Big H' or 'The Great Gordie.' Gordie Howe is Mr. Hockey – a nickname dignified and straight to the point.

Howe, who hailed from Floral, Sask., became the face for hockey and the poster child for excellence and longevity. The New York Rangers had the first crack at him, but he was just 15 years old when he attended their training camp. The bright lights of the Big Apple sent the ultra-shy, homesick teenager packing.

A year later, however, the Detroit Red Wings invited Howe to their training camp in neighboring Windsor, Ont. And after a year in the minors, he began a pro career that eclipsed all others.

Howe's career is about the numbers. He played 1,767 NHL games (26 seasons). His 801 goals and 1,850 points made him the NHL's all-time leading scorer at the time. There were four Stanley Cups, six Hart Trophies as MVP and six scoring titles.

Oh, and he may have inadvertently invented Take Your Child to Work Day.

Howe retired from the NHL after 25 seasons but returned to pro hockey after two years away. He joined the WHA's Houston Aeros along with sons Marty, 19, and Mark, 18. Mrs. Hockey – that is, Howe's wife, Colleen – was the one who engineered the deal, and the Howe men played together for seven seasons: four in Houston, two in New England and a final year in the NHL with the Hartford Whalers.

In 419 WHA games (six seasons), Howe had 174 goals and 508 points and was named MVP in 1973-74. He led the Aeros to championships in his first two WHA seasons.

Howe was 52 when he hung up his skates for good.

Off the ice, Howe was a gentleman: polite, humble and humorous. On the ice, Mr. Hockey was business, as well known for his famous elbows, which he dished out like candies on Halloween, as for his ability to score goals. If the game took a physical turn, Howe was all in, so much so that scoring a goal, drawing an assist and getting into a fight in the same game is known as a Gordie Howe hat trick.

In 1997, *The Hockey News* ranked Howe as the NHL's third-best player of all time.

– By Mike Brophy

15 SAM POLLOCK

SAM POLLOCK HAD one tough act to follow. How does anyone match the accomplishments and influence of Frank Selke, Sr.? Selke helped build Maple Leaf Gardens during The Great Depression and developed farm systems and dynasties alike in Toronto and

Montreal. For Pollock, he created a dynasty of his own and duped the league into allowing him to keep world-class prospects.

Under Selke, the Montreal Canadiens won a record five consecutive Stanley Cups. They didn't reach the final in the four years following, which led to their beloved GM's retirement.

Under Pollock, the Habs won successive Stanley Cups in 1965 and 1966, advanced to the final in 1967 and regained Lord Stanley's mug again in 1968 and 1969. Pol-

lock quickly earned respect from his peers in NHL management and within the league – so much so that he was asked to develop the process for the 1967 expansion draft that welcomed six teams to the NHL.

Pollock's recruiting ability overflowed the Canadiens' farm system with talent. It was thought the club would lose prized prospects, but that never transpired, and Montreal continued to dominate the league. Pollock made his second-year pros available only halfway through the expansion draft, saving Rogie Vachon, Serge Savard, Carol Vadnais, Danny Grant and Jacques Lemaire by adding them to the protected list.

As sponsorship for junior hockey ended, a universal draft was implemented to create an equal playing field for all 12 NHL teams. Although Pollock reportedly proposed a rule preventing teams from trading their picks, the shrewd GM took advantage of new clubs desperate for immediate help. He offered them veterans for first-round draft picks. Montreal would benefit by drafting the likes of Guy Lafleur into their lineup. While the new teams stalled, Montreal soared.

– By Paul Patskou

16 MARIO LEMIEUX

HE MAY NOT be jumping over the boards anymore, but whenever Mario Lemieux enters a room, his presence is as commanding as ever. Part of it is his 6-foot-4 frame. Another is the credit he receives for saving the Pittsburgh Penguins franchise on multiple occasions.

And, of course, a large part is the jaw-dropping skill that carried him to six NHL scoring

titles, three MVP awards and a Conn Smythe Trophy each time he captained Pittsburgh to a Stanley Cup – twice, back-to-back in 1991 and 1992. Despite the injuries and illnesses, including cancer, that kept him short of 1,000 games, when Lemieux retired in 2006 he ranked seventh in league history with 1,723 points, ninth in goals (690) and 10th in assists

(1,033). "There would be no franchise in Pittsburgh without him," said Eddie Johnston, the man who drafted Lemieux first overall in 1984 as Pittsburgh's GM and would later coach him as well.

Long-term deals and deferred payments mortgaged the team's future and landed it in bankruptcy in 1998. Lemieux, then retired, teamed up with billionaire Ron Burkle to buy the Penguins. The team owed Lemieux $32.5 million in deferred salary. Rather than accept cash, he suggested converting the money into equity that gave him control of the franchise.

After saving the Penguins on the ice, Lemieux returned to save the Penguins off it. He became co-owner and chairman and spent his days in the team offices, learning the business side and working to pay back every cent to every creditor.

In December 2000, he came out of retirement, making him a player-owner. And after retiring for good in 2006, Lemieux pulled off another savior-like move: he secured a new arena deal in Pittsburgh, and the Consol Energy Center opened in 2010.

– By Shelly Anderson

17 DON CHERRY

WHEN CONNOR MCDAVID broke his hand during a fight in November 2014, the number of hot takes scorched the media landscape. Everyone was expected to weigh in and NHL players weren't immune.

Milan Lucic was one of them. Given his appetite for truculence, his response was no surprise. "You definitely respect the fact he's willing to step up for himself," Lucic said. "Not contradicting or going against what Don Cherry was saying, it's good to see that a player of his caliber has that fire."

Did you catch that right there? Lucic, a 6-foot-3, 233-pound bruiser who has never been shy about speaking his mind, wanted to make it clear he wasn't trying to run afoul of Cherry, who had stated publicly he didn't think a pure skill player like McDavid should be fighting.

But that's the influence Cherry, now 83, still wields in the hockey world. On a Saturday night at Air Canada Centre in Toronto, you will find the largest concentration of NHL reporters in the English-speaking world. And when *Coach's Corner* comes on during the first intermission, a huge crowd gathers around the TV monitors. Some of those gawkers hate Cherry, others love him, but the crowd is much thinner when other commentators speak.

When Rogers Media won the NHL's exclusive national broadcasting rights in 2013, essentially making Cherry's former employer, the CBC, a ward of the conglomerate, it appeared his days as one of the most notorious hockey broadcast personalities were num-

bered. But in typical 'Grapes' fashion, he stuck it out. Now four years into the deal, *Coach's Corner* is still a *Hockey Night in Canada* staple. But Cherry continues to carry a ton of weight, and he stands by his resume. "I watch hockey every night," he said. "I go to minor midget games, I saw McDavid when he was a bantam, I was coach of the year in the AHL and the NHL. I'm coaching the CHL Top Prospects Game, and I was a player. From April 8 to June 19 in the playoffs, I've been on the air every other night for 34 years. I want somebody to beat that on credentials. I know what I'm talking about."

And lots of folks agree. The most popular YouTube clips of *Coach's Corner* draw views in the six-figure range. Sure, change is constant in the broadcasting landscape, but Cherry still has fun every Saturday night. "Nobody really knew what was going to happen – I was concerned," he said. "But it's even a little better now because I don't have to see anyone. And I have the best opening and closing graphics I've ever had."

Cherry said his studio is sequestered from the other sets, so he just shows up and does his business with little distraction from outside noise. Not that he was against his new compatriots. George Stroumboulopoulos, the man brought in to replace MacLean at the main desk before MacLean reclaimed his position two years later, may have been "a different cat," in Cherry's words, but Grapes also counts him as an ally. That's because Stroumboulopoulos once had former NHL agitator Sean Avery on his talk show and stood up to Avery when his guest trashed Cherry on the air. "I never forgot that," Cherry said. "He's all right in my books."

As for how the new-ish post is going, it depends on who you ask, or rather on who's willing to share their thoughts. After Cherry complained on the air about the amount of time his segment was allotted (a complaint he had raised numerous times in the past with CBC), multiple media outlets conducted polls on Cherry's deployment. Were people happy with less Cherry, or were they outraged that there wasn't more of the colorful commentator? Unfortunately, the question was just a Rorschach test for the newspapers. Left-leaning surveys showed that people were happy, while right-leaning surveys showed that people were outraged.

And it's not like Cherry is changing. He still rocks flamboyant suits, he still goes overboard on occasion (which he readily admits to) and he still has an opinion to deliver.

For example, the man who gave us the Christmas stocking staple *Rock'em Sock'em Hockey* videos now lives in a world where NHL enforcers will need radio tags if they become any more endangered. But as much as Cherry loves hockey's policemen, you can't call him dogmatic when it comes to the issue of fists without talent. "I always believed a guy should be able to play," he said. "If you look at my Boston Bruins teams, John Wensink had 28 goals one year, Stan Jonathan could score 20 and Terry O'Reilly was one of our best players."

Grapes isn't ignorant of the analytics movement, either, even if he believes puck-possession players can be intuited by the best coaches. "Toe Blake, he could tell if a guy had the puck a lot," he said. "Pat Burns, Pat Quinn...they were proud to say they weren't X's and O's guys. I don't think stats knowledge hurts. If you say it's not a big deal, people think you're from a hundred years ago."

Interestingly, Cherry had an anecdote about why players shouldn't care about advanced stats. He said numbers both good and bad have influenced their play and usually for the worse. "I always tried to keep the plus-minus away from the players," Cherry said. "When the numbers came out, I always tried to hide them."

You can wonder when he'll finally cede his spot at the table, but the man sounds content to be where he is today. "People ask me when I'm going to retire. I say, 'Retire from what?' If I get put off, it's been a great run."

– By Ryan Kennedy

18 CONN SMYTHE

IN HIS 1962 autobiography, *Behind the Cheering*, Frank Selke said of Conn Smythe, "It is impossible to imagine what would have happened to professional hockey in Canada had he stayed in New York."

Born and raised in Toronto, Smythe captained his University of Toronto team to the Ontario Hockey Association championship in 1915 and later coached the varsity team when he returned after military service in the First

World War. Smythe's involvement with professional hockey began in 1926 when he was hired to lead the New York Rangers. Before the season started, he was fired because of a conflict with his boss. Smythe took the money he was paid, gambled it successfully, and assembled a syndicate to buy the Toronto St. Pats. Upon taking over on Feb. 14, 1927, he renamed the team the Maple Leafs in honor of the emblem Canadian soldiers had worn during the war.

Serving a few short terms as coach, though mainly as GM and eventually majority owner, Smythe made pro hockey a success in Toronto. He was the driving force behind the construction of Maple Leaf Gardens, which opened at the start of 1931-32. The Leafs won their first Stanley Cup that season, and Smythe would have his name engraved on the trophy seven more times before his tenure with the team ended in 1962.

With a national audience built through Foster Hewitt's radio broadcasts, Smythe used the success of the Leafs to his advantage. He became the NHL's most influential governor and influenced league business. He was elected to the Hall of Fame in 1958, and the NHL introduced a trophy in his name in 1964 to honor the playoff MVP.

– By Eric Zweig

19 HERB BROOKS

IN 1980, HERB Brooks took a bunch of college kids to Lake Placid and beat the powerful U.S.S.R., who had won gold four times in a row at the Olympics. It became known as the Miracle on Ice, and the game still maintains its legendary status. *Sports Illustrated* ranked it No. 1 in its 100 Greatest Moments in Sports History.

The journey wasn't what was most amazing, though. It was Brooks' very belief that it was possible. "I guess that's why he's going to go down in history as one of the greatest coaches of all-time," said Nashville Predators GM David Poile.

Poile's father, Bud Poile, had a hand in helping the Americans prepare for the mighty Soviets. The elder Poile was commissioner of the Central League the year leading up to the Olympics in Lake Placid. He inserted the United States into the schedule, giving the youngsters valuable experience playing against the pros.

Brooks was relentless, often skating his players into the ice when he was unhappy with their efforts. During the Olympics, when Soviet coach Viktor Tikhonov rested some of his top players, Brooks chose otherwise. In the end, he was right.

Despite being crushed 10-3 by the Soviet Union in their final exhibition game, the U.S. was ready. The Soviets built leads of 1-0 and 2-1, but the Americans wouldn't be denied. With the U.S. leading 4-3, ABC's Al Michaels delivered the famous line, "Do you believe in miracles? Yes!"

The U.S. went on to capture the gold medal, beating Finland to complete the miracle.

Brooks was inducted into the Hall of Fame as a builder in 2006. He coached seven seasons in the NHL with the Rangers, North Stars, Devils and Penguins, but is best remembered for leading perhaps the greatest upset in sports. Was it a miracle, or the vision of a genius? "I'd like to give you an answer as to why Brooks thought he could take those kids and win at the Olympics," Poile said. "But isn't that a quality of all the best leaders in the world – their belief?"

– By Mike Brophy

20 ANATOLI TARASOV

AS EARLY AS 1964, Anatoli Tarasov was pushing for NHL clubs to play against the Soviet national team. Muzz Patrick, then GM of the New York Rangers, politely declined because he didn't want to embarrass the world champions by beating the crap out of them. Tarasov's request fell on deaf ears, but eight years later, his wish for a clash of hockey titans became reality, and the Soviets proved beyond a shadow of a doubt they could keep up with Canada's best pros, even though they lost the eight-game Summit Series on a last-minute goal by Paul Henderson.

Tarasov and his colleague Arkady Chernyshov had asked for time off from their jobs as national team coaches six months earlier. Still, even in their absence, it was the innovative tactics and techniques they used to win three Olympic gold medals and nine straight World Championships that made the 1972 team such a tough foe for Canada.

Tarasov and Chernyshov expected to be asked back following their respite, but Soviet Sports Committee officials had other ideas: the two were essentially fired. With Soviet leader Leonid Brezhnev in the house, Tarasov got himself in hot water when he pulled his Red Army club off the ice in the middle of the third period of a game with Spartak to protest the referee's decision to disallow a Red Army goal.

His grandson, Alyosha, told Canadian journalist Matt Fisher of Postmedia News in 2012 that Tarasov denied a request from a Soviet politician to throw a game against Eastern Bloc ally Czechoslovakia at the 1972 Olympics in Japan. The Soviets had already clinched the gold medal, but two points for the Czechoslovaks would have given them the silver medal and relegated the U.S. to bronze.

Tarasov played a large role in the development of Vladislav Tretiak when the legendary goaltender was still in his teens, teaching him to sharpen his reflexes in the off-season by blocking tennis balls hit toward him while moving his feet.

Tarasov valued teamwork. When he coached Red Army, he insisted that every newcomer secure the approval of all other players. His players could pass the puck and put it on their teammates' tape almost blindfolded. He discouraged long individual rushes and convinced them they could save energy by letting the puck do the work.

Known as the father of Soviet hockey, Tarasov was the first Russian to be inducted into the Hall of Fame as a builder. He founded the hockey program at the Central Army Sports Club in Moscow in 1946 and launched the Golden Puck Tournament in 1964, giving more than a million children the opportunity to play organized house-league hockey on outdoor rinks, usually constructed near large apartment complexes.

Many longtime Soviet hockey followers believe that Anatoli Firsov, a player Tarasov developed, was the country's greatest player of all-time. Firsov retired after the 1972 Olympics, and North Americans never saw him play in the Summit Series. Tarasov also tutored Alexander Yakushev and Valeri Kharlamov, who were both outstanding in that series.

Tarasov died on June 23, 1995, at the age of 76.

– By Denis Gibbons

21 FRANK SELKE

FRANK SELKE HELPED build two historic NHL franchises, designing a blueprint for generations of GMs to follow, by focusing on strong farm systems. He was also one of the reasons the Maple Leafs and Canadiens became such fierce rivals. Both clubs had experienced bigger rivalries with other teams in the early days of the NHL, but it wasn't until Selke left Toronto to become GM in Montreal in 1946-47 – and the Leafs and Habs met in the Stanley Cup final for the first time – that the great rivalry between the two was born.

Too small to make it as a player, Selke began managing teams in his hometown of Berlin (Kitchener), Ont., while he was still a teenager. He moved to Toronto in 1917 after a short stint in the army and coached the University of Toronto team. Selke later managed several amateur and professional clubs in Toronto, including the 1929 Memorial Cup champion Toronto Marlboros, before Conn Smythe hired him as assistant GM of the Leafs in October 1929.

There, Selke helped groom such stars as Joe Primeau, Busher Jackson, Charlie Conacher and Red Horner, but he felt his contributions to the team's success during the 1930s were underappreciated. Smythe was unhappy when Selke acquired Ted Kennedy without his permission in 1943, even though Kennedy became a star, so Selke left Toronto in the summer of 1946 and two months later became GM in Montreal. The Leafs achieved great success in the next few years with the young players Selke brought in, but as he built the farm system in Montreal, the Canadiens developed into one of the more successful teams in hockey history.

The NHL created the Selke Trophy, awarded to the league's best defensive forward, in his honor in 1978.

– By Eric Zweig

22 JACK ADAMS

THERE ARE DIVERGING opinions on Jack Adams. Supporters say he built the Detroit Red Wings into an NHL power. His tireless efforts turned the Wings into the only American team capable of battling the Leafs and Canadiens for NHL supremacy during the six-team era. "He planted the seeds that allowed Detroit to blossom as Hockeytown," wrote former Wings commentator Budd Lynch in his autobiography.

Others, mainly former Wings players, insist it was the arrogance and vindictiveness of Adams that destroyed the Detroit dynasty of the mid-1950s and greased the skids for the 'Dead Wings Era' from the late 1960s into the early 1980s. "If he hadn't jerked the roster around, we would have won six or seven Stanley Cups instead of four," said former Wings captain Ted Lindsay.

Adams arrived to take over the Detroit helm in 1927 and reigned over the club through 1962, a span in which the Wings won seven Stanley Cups.

A stern taskmaster and as miserly as they came at contract time, Adams was of the belief that players were interchangeable and that even a championship-caliber club had a shelf life of five years.

This is why he so frequently moved players, a formula that had worked for him in the past but blew up spectacularly when he dealt away half of his 1954-55 Cup winner. "I think he made a big mistake in making such wholesale changes," said former Wing Johnny Wilson in a 1995 interview. "It was still a young team. Most of us were 27 or 28 and we had a few more years of good hockey left."

By 1958-59, just four short years after capturing consecutive Stanley Cups, the Wings were a last-place team, and the players blamed Adams for crushing the chemistry of what had been one of the NHL's best organizations. "We had so many good years left," said former Wing Marty Pavelich.

– By Bob Duff

 ## 23 EDDIE SHORE

IT'S HARD TO decide whether Eddie Shore made a bigger impact on the teams he played for or on the hockey world altogether. But he carved an incredible legacy in more than 50 years of service to the sport. One of the best (and nastiest) defensemen of all time, Shore led the Boston Bruins to their first and second Stanley Cups, won four Hart Trophies and was an eight-time all-star, usually on the first team. Had the Norris Trophy been around in the 1930s, he probably would have earned a bunch of those, too.

Shore's surly, physical style had far-reaching consequences for the game. In 1933, he almost killed Ace Bailey of the Toronto Maple Leafs with a hit from behind. Doctors were able to relieve the pressure on Bailey's brain and save his life, but he never played in the NHL again. To help Bailey's financial situation, the league held an All-Star Game, which began a mid-season tradition that continues to this day (though it is no longer charitable in that sense).

Shore was also a businessman and a coach. He bought the AHL's Springfield Indians in 1939 and became their coach. At one point, he even played for the Indians and the NHL's New York Americans in the same season, but he retired a few years later.

Shore was astute in arena management, too. He helped found the Ice Capades along with nine other arena owners and moved several times in the AHL. When the AHL wanted a team to play in Syracuse's bigger arena in 1951, Shore took ownership. But Springfield always beckoned, and he was back in Massachusetts after three seasons. "He lost $500,000 in Syracuse," said his son Ted. "Springfield had more events – high school hockey, public skating, the Ice Capades."

Although he had a lot of savvy off the ice, Shore was also a taskmaster and the definition of old school. "He was tough," said Ted, who did everything from taking tickets to shovelling snow to coaching when his father

ran the Indians. "Meaning that if you didn't do your job, you'd hear from him. 'Take care of it,' 'Make it work' – that's what I remember. He was tough but fair. 'If you have a better way, I'll listen, but in the meantime, do it my way.' "

Shore was also responsible for bringing his own nephew into the game. Jack Butterfield was just home from the Second World War and the Royal Canadian Air Force in England when the elder Shore put him to work. By 1966, after a decade as the Indians' GM, Butterfield was named president of the AHL. He kept that post until 1994 then served as chairman of the board of governors until he died in 2010.

Not all of Shore's employees had positive memories, however. His unorthodox and strict management styles caused a coup d'etat in 1966, when his players complained of unjust suspensions and paycheques withheld for spurious reasons. The players brought in lawyer Alan Eagleson as a defense, and Shore eventually sold the team to the Los Angeles Kings, only to buy it back seven years later. That incident sparked Eagleson and pro players in both the AHL and NHL to establish unions. With Ted Lindsay and Doug Harvey putting in work since the late 1950s, the NHLPA was formed in 1967, with Eagleson as executive director.

In the end, Shore was a man of many roles. He was a player and an owner, a hero and a villain, and one of the best to ever play the game. For better or worse, he was relentless in everything he did.

– By Ryan Kennedy

24 LESTER PATRICK

LESTER PATRICK'S CAREER was one of the longest and most diverse in hockey. He was responsible for more innovations, positive rule changes and miscellaneous improvements in the game than any other personality. The penalty shot, numbers on players' jerseys, the assist and forward passing are all marks that Patrick's ingenuity left on the game.

Patrick was the first defenseman to regularly lug the puck out of his own zone and deep into enemy territory. That happened in 1902 when he played for a team in Brandon, Man. "Instinct and temperament proved too strong for Lester," said Elmer Ferguson of the *Montreal Herald.* "He felt that a defensemen should do more than defend, so he rushed the puck as well."

That was just the first of many Patrick innovations. He felt it was foolish for defensemen to stand in front of each other like in lacrosse and cover point players, thinking it was wiser to have defensemen lined up abreast. Once again, his imprint was indelibly etched in hockey strategy.

A Hall of Fame player, Patrick helped build a chain of rinks that led to the formation of the Pacific Coast Hockey Association, most notably in Victoria, Vancouver, Seattle, Edmonton, Calgary, Regina and Saskatoon. When the New York Rangers fired Conn Smythe before the 1926-27 season, Patrick was named coach-GM. He went on to win Stanley Cups in 1928 and 1933 in his dual role, and then another in 1940 as GM with Frank Boucher behind the bench.

As a retired 44-year-old defenseman, Patrick once again became a part of hockey history. In the 1928 playoffs, when his goalie, Lorne Chabot, was seriously injured during the Stanley Cup final with the Montreal Maroons, Patrick put on the pads to play goal for the Blueshirts and defeated the favored Maroons. "This dramatic moment," wrote *Toronto Sun* columnist Trent Frayne, "has become a part of the lore of the sport, as legendary in hockey as the World Series home run Babe Ruth hit off Charlie Root of the Chicago Cubs when he pointed to the distant center field bleachers and then laced the ball there."

– By Stan Fischler

25 BORJE SALMING

BORJE SALMING WASN'T the first Swede to play in the NHL. He wasn't even the first player from Sweden to attend a Toronto Maple Leafs training camp. But he was the first to make an impact.

In the 1970s, Swedish players were perceived to be all skill, no aggression. However, when Maple Leafs scout Gerry McNamara ventured to Sweden to look at the talented Inge Hammarstrom, another skater challenged his deep-seated assumptions. This other player wasn't just tremendously gifted. He had just been ejected for rough play. This was during the days of regular brawls and the Broad Street Bullies, so overseas players arriving in North America needed to survive the rough-and-tumble years after expansion. Swedish sensation Ulf Sterner couldn't hack it in the 1960s with the New York Rangers, but Salming proved fearless.

Both Salming and Hammarstrom signed with Toronto and attended training camp in September 1973. Their fellow Leafs were incredulous. In two long strides, Salming could cross from one blueline to the other at tremendous speed. Both newcomers were talented, but their ability to react to intimidation was questioned. The answer came quickly. Their second game of the season was against the roughest bunch of all: Philadelphia. While Hammarstrom shied away from physicality, Salming refused to be intimidated, even fighting tough guy Dave 'The Hammer' Schultz to a draw.

Salming and his game-changing skills were targeted the next few years, but he continued

to dispel the notion that Swedes were soft. After Mel Bridgman attacked Salming in the infamous Leafs-Flyers playoff series in 1976, 'The King,' as Salming was known by then, scored a highlight reel breakaway goal against Philadelphia's Bernie Parent the next game, earning one of the loudest standing ovations ever heard at Maple Leaf Gardens. A few months later, in a show of devotion to their beloved blueliner, fans at the Gardens gave Salming another standing ovation when he was introduced as a member of Sweden at the inaugural Canada Cup in Toronto.

Salming excelled in the NHL's most brutal era. In the process, he helped pave the way for other Swedish players.

– By Paul Patskou

26 JOHN ZIEGLER JR.

HE WAS, PERHAPS, better known for his natty attire and trademark yellow ties. But as NHL president from 1977 to 1992, John Ziegler Jr. directed the league from near-ruin to prosperity during its most precarious modern period. He rarely received proper credit and respect for his accomplishments, however, since his low-key, personal approach favored negotiations and building consensus among owners rather than ruling by decree.

When Ziegler, the Red Wings' lawyer and alternate governor, succeeded Clarence Campbell, only a handful of NHL clubs were profitable, and the league itself was insolvent. By stabilizing tottering NHL franchises and then brokering the end of the NHL-WHA conflict, he ended the chaos and fiscal hemorrhaging.

Engineering the absorption of four WHA teams while the others vanished (he termed it "an expansion that was really a contraction"), Ziegler ushered in an era of prosperity during which most NHL teams reversed their fortunes. New league-wide attendance records were set annually, laying the foundation for today's unprecedented growth.

Part of the turnaround was what Ziegler often called the "special relationship" between the owners and the NHLPA. The threesome of Ziegler and two more voluble men – Bill Wirtz, Chicago Blackhawks owner and chairman of the NHL board of governors, and the infamous NHLPA head Alan Eagleson – dominated the league's business decisions the way Wayne Gretzky dominated the ice.

Although he struggled at times with his own public image, as well as the NHL's, the league in Ziegler's era was unjustly criticized for lacking innovation. His NHL pioneered placing big league sports on cable TV, both nationally and regionally, after the broadcast networks backed away. Similarly, the All-Star weekend format, the NHL Awards program, the move of the June entry draft to different cities and the launch of video review all began during Ziegler's tenure.

– By Stu Hackel

27 JAMES NORRIS

WHEN THE TORONTO Maple Leafs had trouble signing Frank Mahovlich to a new contract in 1962, Chicago Black Hawks owner James Norris mentioned to new Leafs ownership partner Harold Ballard at a cocktail party that he'd pay Toronto a million dollars for the rights to 'The Big M.' Norris peeled off 10 hundred-dollar bills as a down payment, and Ballard quickly accepted. An agreement was written and signed on a cocktail napkin.

The next morning, newspapers screamed that it was the biggest deal in sports history. But when Hawks GM Tommy Ivan went to Maple Leaf Gardens to deliver Norris' check for $1 million, Leafs brass reneged and the deal collapsed. It was a rare instance of Norris not getting his way.

His greatest fame – or infamy – in sports came from his monopolistic control over boxing from the late 1940s to the early 1960s, which included charges of match-fixing and his association with organized crime figures. His dominance in hockey was also quite profound. Norris owned the Hawks but also co-owned the Detroit Olympia and Madison Square Garden, which in turn owned the Detroit Red Wings and New York Rangers. He also wielded influence over the Boston Bruins and Boston Garden, the owner of which, Charles Adams, owed a large unpaid debt to Norris. Critics nicknamed the NHL the 'Norris House League.'

Chicago was talent-poor when Norris and partner Arthur Wirtz took control (covertly in 1946, openly by 1952), and he persuaded the other clubs to ship him players on friendly terms. Bodies seemed to move most freely between the powerful Red Wings, owned by his half-brother, Bruce, and the Hawks. Not surprisingly, both preferred players to be submissive and were leading opponents of the nascent players' union in the mid-1950s.

Chicago finally won the Stanley Cup in 1961 with the help of ex-Wings everywhere. GM Tommy Ivan had been Detroit's coach, and star goalie Glenn Hall and reliable defenseman Al Arbour played major roles, as did Ted Lindsay, once Detroit's fiery captain. Banished to Chicago for his union involvement, Lindsay retired in 1960 after mentoring a new crop of Hawks youngsters, including Stan Mikita.

When the NHL announced expansion plans in 1966, St. Louis was awarded a franchise even though no ownership group had bid for a club. But Norris and Wirtz owned the St. Louis Arena, which they wanted to unload. The league accommodated them.

– By Stu Hackel

28 ART ROSS

AS A MAN who played almost his entire career before the NHL was formed, Art Ross wasn't just one of the best players. He was also one of the most influential.

Back when defensemen were known as two different positions, "point" and "cover point," Ross was a star. In an era of amateurs, he was a professional. He was occasionally used as a hired gun brought in by teams for important games, often holding out for higher salaries when anything above $1,000 was considered almost obscene.

Ross held strong opinions on the rules of the game. He was an early advocate when the National Hockey Association eliminated the rover. And although he always kept himself in excellent physical condition, he believed in frequent substitutions when most people still expected star players to play a full 60 minutes. Goalie Clint Benedict is often credited with being the reason the NHL allowed goalies to drop to the ice to make saves during its inaugural season in 1917-18, but Ross had been lobbying for the change for nearly a year, having approved of the rule his friends Frank and Lester Patrick had introduced earlier in the Pacific Coast Hockey Association.

In 1924, Ross was hired as the first coach, GM and vice-president of the Boston Bruins. He quickly built the team into a perennial power and led the Bruins for 30 years.

Through his role on the NHL rules committee, Ross introduced many modern innovations. He redesigned the pucks and nets that all leagues soon used, invented some of the earliest helmets and introduced icing to curb delaying tactics. He donated a trophy for the NHL scoring leader in 1948 and was inducted into the Hall of Fame in 1949.

– By Eric Zweig

# LORD STANLEY

WE'LL NEVER KNOW what might have happened otherwise, but Lord Stanley's donation of a championship trophy – first announced at a sports dinner in Ottawa on March 18, 1892 – was the catalyst that pushed hockey in Canada from regional pastime to national passion.

Because of the need for cold weather to make ice, as well as the weeklong travel across the country by train, hockey leagues in the 19th century were small, with short schedules, and locally based. Hockey was played and followed most ardently in the Quebec-Ontario corridor, sections of the Maritimes and around Winnipeg. It spread across the nation, but nothing linked the dispersed interests together. Lord Stanley's gift didn't connect the regions immediately, but by the end of 1896 – after the Winnipeg Victorias challenged and defeated the Montreal Victorias in February, only to lose a rematch in December – challenge matches for the Stanley Cup were Canadian news from coast to coast.

Frederick Arthur Stanley was born in London, England on Jan. 15, 1841. His father served three terms as prime minister of England, and Stanley followed him into politics, eventually serving in the House of Lords as Baron Stanley of Preston. An avid sportsman, he was appointed Governor General of Canada in 1888 and quickly fell in love with the many winter activities the country offered. After attending his first hockey game at the Montreal Winter Carnival on Feb. 4, 1889, his children became passionate about the sport.

The championship trophy Lord Stanley purchased in England for 10 guineas was first awarded in 1893. Engraved with the name "Dominion Hockey Challenge Cup," it became known as the Stanley Cup right away. Although Lord Stanley returned to England before his trophy was presented, he named two Canadian trustees to oversee its competition. Philip Dansken Ross and later William Foran worked hard to ensure that the Stanley Cup remained the highest honor in hockey. Despite the protests of amateur enthusiasts, they agreed to open the competition to professional teams in 1906, and when the two top pro leagues organized their own "World Series" in 1913-14, the trustees agreed to end the trophy's original challenge concept. This helped pave the way for the NHL to make the Stanley Cup the symbol it is today.

– By Eric Zweig

30 GARY DAVIDSON

THE PRO-ESTABLISHMENT SEGMENT of North American sports leagues looks upon the legacy of Gary Davidson as that of a rabble-rousing militant lawyer out to cause nothing but headaches. The free-market opportunists in the crowd bow to him in deference.

Davidson, 83, is a retired Santa Ana, Calif., lawyer who established the boardroom equivalent of a Gordie Howe hat trick in his practicing prime. In a seven-year span, Davidson spearheaded rival leagues to spring up in basketball, hockey and football. In 1967, he cofounded the American Basketball Association and served as its first president. The ABA competed with the NBA for nine years until they merged in 1976.

In 1972, having never watched a hockey game in his life, Davidson became a powerful force in the creation of the WHA, which competed with the NHL for seven years until they merged in 1979. And partway through both ventures, Davidson was the founder and first commissioner of the World Football League, which lasted just the 1974 season and part of 1975.

In short, Davidson saw opportunity and pounced.

On the hockey front, he was approached by promoter Dennis Murphy in 1971 and told that what he was doing with the ABA was inspirational to him and a few of his business associates. The compliment worked. "Dennis came to me and said, 'You know, Gary, there's only one league in hockey,' and I said 'Oh, let's start another one,'" Davidson told *The Hockey News* in 2010. "I had never seen a hockey game, though. Three guys from Canada (Bill Hunter, Ben Hatskin and John Bassett) then came down to meet with me. The next thing you know, the NHL was trying to shut us down. They tried to crush us from the get-go. They sued us in every city they had a franchise and we had a franchise – and we countersued for antitrust and won."

Davidson and the WHA didn't hesitate to battle the NHL head-to-head, naming New York, Boston, Toronto and Chicago as locations for its 12-team launch in 1972. That spring, the upstart league started operating as though it controlled the landscape with little regard for the NHL. It held a player draft and soon Toronto Maple Leafs goalie Bernie

Parent was the first player to announce that he'd be playing in the WHA the next fall. That opened the floodgate for the likes of Bobby Hull, Derek Sanderson, Ted Green and J.C. Tremblay to sign lucrative deals in the fledgling league.

Eventually financial instability caught up with the WHA, and it was forced to fold in 1979. But its four strongest teams – Edmonton, New England (Hartford), Quebec and Winnipeg – were absorbed by the NHL.

– By Brian Costello

31 CARL BREWER

IT WOULD BE easy to dismiss Carl Brewer as a malcontent, an eccentric who questioned management at every turn. Brewer, however, was much more than that.

A fast, talented and scrappy defenseman, Brewer was a key member of the Toronto Maple Leafs teams that won three straight Stanley Cups from 1962 to 1964. But Brewer wasn't a team player in an era when NHL owners ran their clubs like factories. His best work wasn't in the corners of the rink but in the corridors of power, and he took pity on no one.

Brewer was always different. He once cut out the palms of his gloves so he could hold his stick shaft with his bare hands and grab opponents' jerseys without being detected. He was even better at antagonizing management, and this is where he made his greatest contribution to hockey.

After he retired for a third time, Brewer was shocked and angered when he discovered his annual pension after 12 years in the NHL would only be $6,200. He began writing letters and asking questions, and he wound up spearheading a suit against the league over the pension issue. His legacy is the 1991 landmark lawsuit against the NHL that won players of his generation $40 million in pension money.

Brewer died in 2001, and dozens of those same players he helped secure an improved pension for attended his funeral. "The players were screwed for too long," Brewer said a couple months before he died. "Someone had to step up, and I did."

– By Alan Adams

32 FRANK PATRICK

FOR DECADES, THE NHL rulebook carried up to 22 pieces of legislation introduced by Frank Patrick. As of today, these changes still stand.

After Frank, along with his brother Lester, starred on the Renfrew Millionaires in 1910, the Patricks created the Pacific Coast Hockey Association in 1911-12 and introduced most of the rules that modernized hockey. Frank spearheaded the idea of creating blue lines to introduce forward passing, first in the neutral zone and later everywhere on the ice. He was instrumental in the PCHA introducing penalty shots, creating a modern playoff system and allowing goaltenders to drop to the ice to make saves.

Having owned, coached, managed and starred for the PCHA's Vancouver Millionaires, who won the Stanley Cup in 1915, Frank served as managing director of the

NHL in 1933-34. He later worked for the Boston Bruins and the Montreal Canadiens.

– By Eric Zweig

33 HOWIE MORENZ

WHEN DESCRIBING HOWIE Morenz's influence on early professional hockey, what sounds like tired old hyperbole or cliché is actually truth. He was the best player of the first half of the 20th century. He was hockey's first superstar.

That's how he was billed when the expansion New York Americans began their inaugural season at a brand new Madison Square Garden in 1925. MSG owner Tex Rickard insisted their first opponent be the Montreal

Canadiens, featuring Howie Morenz, the man who had inspired him to buy a hockey team.

Born in Mitchell, Ont., Morenz moved with his family to nearby Stratford, where he quickly caught the attention of professional teams. He slipped through the fingers of the Toronto St. Patricks and signed with the Canadiens. It's difficult to imagine in today's NHL that a 5-foot-9, 165-pound player could dominate the league, but that's exactly what Morenz did.

In some ways he was an innovator. Morenz's style of play attracted crowds when professional hockey was still in its infancy. He was elusive and his dekes unprecedented, and his speed gave opponents fits, leading to his two nicknames: 'The Stratford Streak' and 'The Mitchell Meteor.' In 1928, he became the first player to reach 50 points in a season, when he finished with 51 in 43 games to win his first Hart Trophy.

Morenz starred in Montreal for 11 consecutive seasons, leading the team in points seven times and winning three Stanley Cups, before two less fruitful years split between the Chicago Black Hawks and the New York Rangers. He attempted a triumphant return to the Canadiens in 1936-37, but it was short-lived and tragic.

During a Jan. 28, 1937, game against the Black Hawks, Morenz skated into the corner and his skate got stuck in the boards. Chicago defenseman Earl Seibert checked Morenz and fell on top of him, breaking his leg in four places and ending Morenz's career. Weeks later, he died due to blood clots in his injured leg. His longtime teammate and friend Aurele Joliat said Morenz died of a broken heart.

Morenz's death shook the hockey world. He lay in state at the Montreal Forum where 200,000 people passed his casket to pay their respects. Another 15,000 attended his funeral at the Forum. In the following season, Morenz became the first Hab to have his number retired. Days after the Canadiens raised No. 7 to the rafters, a team of NHL all-stars played against a joint Canadiens-Maroons team in a charity game benefitting Morenz's family. It predates the first official NHL All-Star Game by a decade.

Morenz's legacy and impact on the NHL extended further. His daughter, Marlene, married Bernie 'Boom Boom' Geoffrion. In 1979-80, their son Danny, Morenz's grandson, played 32 games for the Canadiens. In 2011, Blake Geoffrion, Morenz's great-grandson, became a fourth-generation Canadien when he suited up for 13 games.

When Morenz died, he was the NHL's all-time leading scorer with 472 points. He was a three-time Stanley Cup champion and a three-time Hart Trophy winner. He has an arena named after him in Montreal, as well as a street in Stratford, and in 1998 he was ranked No. 15 on *The Hockey News'* list of the 100 Greatest Players. In 1945, he was a member of Hall of Fame's inaugural 12-player induction class.

– By Ian Denomme

 **VIACHESLAV FETISOV** ———

THE QUESTION IS asked and the telephone line goes quiet. Viacheslav 'Slava' Fetisov doesn't believe in speaking ill of the dead. Even when that dead person once arranged to have him handcuffed to a car battery in Kiev. Even when that dead person made his rather charmed life miserable when he drove Fetisov out of the game for a time and almost derailed his dream of playing in the NHL. But mores are mores, and Fetisov isn't about to violate them. In 2014, when asked how he felt when he found out Viktor Tikhonov, the

notorious tyrannical coach of the Soviet national team and Fetisov's personal nemesis, died at 84, he said, "In the Russian doxology, in the religion, when a man dies, you can say good stuff or nothing," Fetisov said. "And that's why I'm not going to talk about it."

Interviewing Fetisov, the greatest defenseman, if not the greatest all-around player Russia has produced, can be a battle of wills. He is at times charming and engaging, at times belligerent and condescending. One minute he admonishes his questioner for not doing his research, the next he's inviting him to Moscow for a tour to see how things have changed for the better.

Fetisov's personality was on full display in the critically acclaimed documentary *Red Army*, which premiered in 2014 and was released to select theaters in 2015. Director Gabe Polsky was first told he could only have 15 minutes with Fetisov for the film and ended up spending 18 hours over three days with him. That made Fetisov the de facto star of the film, which uses his long and tiring battle with Tikhonov and the former Soviet Politburo over his release to the NHL as the backdrop for an examination of the Big Red Machine and how it was used to demonstrate the might of the Soviet Union during the Cold War. The documentary features incredible footage of early Russian hockey under Anatoli Tarasov, Tikhonov's predecessor, but it's Fetisov who steals the show with his candid and sometimes shocking portrayal of life under the constant surveillance of Tikhonov.

On one hand, Fetisov wonders what the fuss is about. He claims that much of the material in the documentary was covered in a book he wrote in 1997. Much of it has been discussed in newspapers and magazines in Russia, and his feud with Tikhonov and the

Soviet system is a well-mined subject. "You never asked me when I came in 1989 about what was happening," Fetisov said. "It wasn't interesting. I went through a tough time, but you didn't give a s---, and now you want to talk about it 25 years later, but it's OK."

Fetisov, 58, speaks on a night when he has just returned from playing beer league hockey in Moscow with former stars Valeri Kamensky, Alexei Kasatonov and Alexei Zhamnov – and some Russian politicians – but that's hardly an isolated event. He still gets on the ice four times a week and claims to have taught Russian president Vladimir Putin to skate.

The ironic thing about the man who helped change the landscape by leaving the Soviet Union for the NHL on his terms is that Fetisov is now part of the levers of power in Russia as a senator in the Federal Assembly. The same man who devoted much of his career to gaining freedom from the oppressive regime is now part of a government that restricts the rights of its LGBT population and ordered an invasion of Ukraine and the annexation of Crimea. At times, Fetisov talks about his work as the Putin-appointed minister of sport and how he managed to get the president on board with reviving sports programs, while at others he does everything he can to distance himself from Putin, who, like Tikhonov, was a former KGB agent.

That gets Fetisov's back up. He points out that George H.W. Bush was once the director of the C.I.A. When it's brought up to him that his president seems to be quashing liberties for the LGBT community and Ukraine with strong-arm tactics, the same kinds of tactics to which he was subjected when trying to gain freedom, he bristles. "I don't work for (Putin), I work for the f---ing government,"

Fetisov said. "I'm not the f---ing main guy to decide what's going on around here. I'm not his friend. I was appointed as a minister, and I met him a few times, and he talked about what we needed to do for sport, and he gave me a job. But I can't call him and go to his *dacha* and talk to him. I'd like to, but I can't. I'm not a puppet, I'm a politician, and the only reason I'm in politics is I try to change what's going on."

Fetisov's influence and imprint on Russian hockey is as indelible during his post-playing career as it was when he captained the Red Army and Russian national teams. After assembling the bronze medal-winning Russian squad in Salt Lake City in 2002, Fetisov accepted Putin's invitation to become the minister of sport and was charged with the challenge of reviving the country's sagging athletic infrastructure. Fetisov boasts that because of his Putin-supported initiatives, 4,000 new sports facilities, including 300 new indoor arenas, were built during his tenure, which lasted until 2008. Athletes former and current have seen improved salaries and pensions. Fetisov was one of the founding members of the KHL and was a key part of the bid committee that landed the 2014 Olympics for Sochi.

Fetisov is the only person in Russia who has both an asteroid (Asteroid 8806, renamed Fetisov) and an arena (Fetisov Arena in Vladivostok) named after him. He asserted that he's the only person in Russia with a building named after him while he's still alive, too. "I'm proud of what I did," Fetisov said. "We raised the budget for sport 20 times, and sport is now a priority for the country. We got the money, we got support from business and government. I did a good job."

At one point in the film, Polsky shows a scene from a local Washington television station that has Alex Ovechkin taking shots at Russian dolls filled with Russian salad dressing hanging from the crossbar of a hockey net. As Ovechkin hits the dolls and the dressing spews, Fetisov says, "We lost our spirit. We lost our pride. We lost our soul."

Fetisov talks about how he tried to help regain that pride through his efforts in the Russian sports system, saying the 1990s and the dawn of the 21st century were a dark time for Russia. But he said Putin has done a lot to restore Russia's pride and, along with it, some order.

As for the documentary, it was a smash hit at Cannes before receiving rave reviews at film festivals in Toronto and New York. But it wasn't among the 15 films shortlisted for the best documentary prize at the 2015 Academy Awards, prompting the founder of Sony Pictures Classics, Tom Bernard, to slam the academy for being too old and stodgy. "Gabe Polsky did a good job and it's a good story," Fetisov said. "It's too bad it got kicked out of the Stanley Cup final for movies. It's too bad, and I think it's politics. Probably there are people who don't want to see it."

– By Ken Campbell

35 PATRICK ROY

PATRICK ROY WASN'T just a trendsetter. He was an icon. His mastery of the butterfly inspired a legion of young goaltenders to emulate him.

When Roy first came to prominence in the 1986 playoffs, his results were undeniable. As a rookie, Roy led the Montreal Canadiens over the Calgary Flames in the 1986 final for his first Stanley Cup. Seven years later, against the Los Angeles Kings, he did it again. Roy, by this time known as 'St. Patrick,' had achieved beatification in Montreal.

All that changed when Mario Tremblay became Canadiens coach in 1995-96. He left Roy in for nine goals during an 11-1 shellacking from Detroit. When Tremblay finally gave him the hook, Roy went over to club president Ronald Corey and told him he'd just played his last game for Montreal.

True to his word, Roy never played for the Habs again. He was dealt to Denver, where he became the bellwether stopper for the Colorado Avalanche, winning two more Stanley Cups in 1996 and 2001.

During his career, Roy won the Conn Smythe and Vezina three times apiece. Among goalies, he finished second in games played (1,026) and wins (551) behind Martin Brodeur, but he remains first in playoff games (247) and playoff wins (151).

But Roy's legacy lives on in the butterfly he bequeathed to his fellow goaltenders, who have since honed it to near perfection. It has gone through numerous tweaks since he introduced it to the NHL three decades ago, but the philosophy remains the same: cover the bottom of the net and force players to shoot high. Aside from Jacques Plante, no other goalie has changed the position more than Roy.

– By Stan Fischler

36 VIKTOR TIKHONOV

VIKTOR TIKHONOV OFTEN stayed up around the clock analyzing the notes he made during matches in a little black book that resembled a Bible. He used the information to coach the Soviet national team to three Olympic gold medals and eight World Championship golds, as well as the 1981 Canada Cup title.

Along the way he created the national team's first famous Russian Five unit of Igor Larionov, Sergei Makarov, Vladimir Krutov, Slava Fetisov and Alexei Kasatonov, all of whom later played in the NHL. The five stars were named to the first all-star team as a unit at the World Championships of 1983 and 1986.

The harsh system Tikhonov employed was the subject of lengthy debates, however. Players were compelled to live in military-like dormitories, unable to see their families for weeks at a time. Contrary to popular belief, opposition to Tikhonov's harsh system wasn't unanimous. In an interview at the 2012 KHL All-Star Game in Latvia, wife of former national team defenseman Alexei Gusarov, Sandra Gusarov, said, "Of course I missed my husband when the players were away living in the barracks. But that was Viktor's style, and guess what? It worked."

Tikhonov himself conceded that the biggest mistake of his career was removing Vladislav Tretiak at the end of the first period of the Soviets' game against the U.S. at the 1980 Olympics in Lake Placid.

Tikhonov was named to the IIHF Hall of Fame as a builder in 1998 and also received the Order of Lenin, the highest honor bestowed by his country. He died in November 2014 at the age of 84.

– By Denis Gibbons

 **BILL WIRTZ**

HOW DISLIKED WAS Bill Wirtz among Chicago Blackhawks fans? In 2007, fans booed when a moment of silence in Wirtz's memory was requested at the United Center.

Wirtz ran the Blackhawks for 41 years, and his penny-pinching leadership earned him the nickname 'Dollar Bill.' He was the last NHL owner not to allow home games to be televised. The other Original Six teams relinquished that ghost in the 1950s. Even his son, current Hawks owner Rocky Wirtz, could only shake his head at his father's fractured logic. "I'd say, 'Dad, we're losing generations of fans by not televising home games,' " Rocky Wirtz told the *New York Times*. "He said it wouldn't be fair to our

fans with season tickets. But we'd gotten down to 3,400 season tickets, which meant maybe 1,500 to 1,700 fans. So we weren't televising home games for (the sake of) 1,700 people? Why bang your head against the wall?"

In 2004, ESPN named the Blackhawks the worst franchise in North American profes-sional sports. Since Wirtz's 2007 death, the Blackhawks, who hadn't lifted Lord Stanley's mug since 1961, have won three Cups with Rocky Wirtz operating an NHL version of *Seinfeld's* Opposite Day. "He would not have agreed with a thing we've done," Rocky Wirtz said.

– By Bob Duff

38 MURRAY COSTELLO

IN A CAREER that spanned half a century, Murray Costello played every role in hockey – player, executive, scout, arbitrator, administrator and visionary.

After a fledging professional career, Costello moved to the amateur level, where he made arguably his greatest impact. In 1979, as president of the Canadian Amateur Hockey Association, he helped shape Canada's success on the world stage. Costello created the Program of Excellence, started its highly successful coaching program and another designed to improve officiating standards for referees. He was instrumental in skill development and the implementation of videos as a teaching tool.

Costello led the merger of CAHA and Hockey Canada, and he represented Canada at the IIHF. He sat on various committees and has been an IIHF council member since 1998. "I have a lot of respect for Murray," said Rene Fasel, IIHF president. "He has done so much. He has always offered me great advice. He has helped me very much."

Costello was also a driving force for the growth of women's hockey and its inclusion in the Winter Olympics. His reach extended far outside Canada, too. He worked with USA

Hockey to establish the U.S. as a hockey nation and was awarded USA Hockey's Wayne Gretzky International Award.

Costello also helped block former NHL president Gil Stein's induction into the Hall of Fame after Stein attempted to orchestrate his own entry. "It's his values," said Edmonton Oilers executive Bob Nicholson, who worked with Costello for more than a decade as president of Hockey Canada. "His values are what you want values for kids in sport to be. He is in it for the right reasons."

– By Alan Adams

39 THE MOLSON FAMILY

GEOFF MOLSON

AFTER SENATOR HARTLAND Molson purchased the Montreal Canadiens with his brother Thomas in September 1957, he was thrust into turmoil during the NHL players' first attempts at organizing a union. Toronto's Conn Smythe told the players to "jump in the lake," and hostility among the owners produced a $3-million antitrust lawsuit filed by the players' attorney. Senator Molson, whose brewery was unionized, took a different stance: he spoke with his players to better understand their concerns. Eventually, he won over the owners, leading to compromises with the players and de-escalation in February 1958.

While playing a big role in strengthening the players' pension fund and helping launch the Hall of Fame, the Molsons' contribution to promoting the game is immeasurable. Molson Breweries sponsored *Hockey Night in Canada*, and by 1976 Molson's Beer was the show's main sponsor, becoming the title sponsor in 1988.

In the mid-1960s, the family's next generation – David, Peter and William – took control of the Canadiens. As president, David became a major advocate for NHL expansion, along with Rangers governor William Jennings. The pair led the expansion committee, and with Molson drafting the blueprint the league agreed to add six clubs for 1967.

David also shared Hartland's affinity for his players. He danced the bunny hop with them at one of the five Stanley Cup parties his club celebrated during his tenure.

The Molson family sold the team in 1971, but Molson Breweries acquired the club in 1978. After selling in 2001, the company retained a minority share with Geoff Molson, representing it on the club's board. In 2009, he formed a partnership led by a third generation of Molsons to buy the Habs.

There was no better evidence of the Molsons' swagger in the hockey world than their company's 1998 beer commercial mocking the new-era NHL with its glowing pucks and non-traditional markets, after the league awarded a rival brewery the *Hockey Night in Canada* title sponsorship. In 2011, the Molson-Coors Brewery recaptured that prize and became the NHL's official beer in North America.

– By Stu Hackel

HARTLAND MOLSON

JAMES CREIGHTON

40 JAMES CREIGHTON

HOCKEY WASN'T INVENTED in any one place at any one time but evolved over centuries.

Modern hockey was preceded by on-ice activities under names like "hurley," "hurling," "bandy," "shinty" and "shinny." Most began as field games in Europe but moved to frozen lakes and rivers when cold weather permitted. Some of these games are recorded in history as early as the 1600s.

Many hockey historians point to a game played inside Montreal's Victoria Skating Rink on March 3, 1875, as the birthplace of organized hockey. The game played that day had some recognizable features for current hockey fans, but there was little about it that was truly modern. There were similar games played in England earlier in the 1870s that were just as organized. Still, as authors Carl Giden, Patrick Houda and Jean-Patrice Martel note in their 2014 book *On the Origin of Hockey*, "The strength of the Montreal claim is that, from that first game, hockey became increasingly structured, at an accelerated pace, thanks in large part to the early work, enthusiasm and 'marketing' know-how of James Creighton."

Creighton is often credited with being the inventor or father of modern hockey, though he never made such claims for himself. Born on June 12, 1850, in Halifax, N.S., where early hockey-like games were played, Creighton moved to Montreal in 1872 and later attended McGill University. There, he taught some friends how to play the version of hockey that he knew. He organized the 1875 game and captained one of the two teams that day. After Montreal newspapers reported on it, Creighton played in nearly every recorded game in the city over the next few years as the sport began to develop a following. The first published Montreal Rules in 1877 were almost identical to field hockey, and Creighton, who also played rugby, likely pushed for the onside rule that banned forward passing.

On March 3, 1882, Creighton was appointed law clerk to the senate in Ottawa. He continued playing hockey there, and along with two sons of Governor General Lord Stanley, he became a key member of the Rideau Rebels when the team was formed in 1889. The Rebels helped promote hockey as the game spread across Canada.

– By Eric Zweig

41 WILLIAM JENNINGS

THERE'S A CRUEL irony in the legacy of Bill Jennings: hockey people will forever associate his name with a lack of goals. Every June for the past 34 years, two goaltenders dressed in tuxedos walk to the stage at the NHL Awards ceremony to collect a piece of hardware awarded to them because they allowed so few goals. It's called the William M. Jennings Trophy.

Funny thing is, Jennings had many goals, and he mostly pursued the ones hardest to attain. He had clairvoyant foresight, vision and drive. So to name an award after him that put "goals" and "fewest" in the same sentence is, good intentions aside, rather unfortunate.

On the other hand, maybe it's appropriate. As a boy, Jennings saw goals evaporate before his very eyes. Born in New York City, Jennings was eight when the stock market crash of 1929 triggered The Great Depression. During the next decade, he watched as financial despair destroyed once-affluent neighbors. He saw the fathers of his childhood friends lose their jobs and resort to relying on food stamps to feed hungry mouths. Through it all, Jennings kept his focus, studied hard and was fortunate enough to have his family send him to Princeton University in New Jersey. From there, the goal-driven young man advanced to Yale Law School.

As an Ivy League-trained lawyer in the late 1940s, Jennings was eager to move back to Manhattan, where he became a partner at the law firm of Simpson, Thacher and Bartlett. He was 38 when his firm was hired to handle the transaction involving the Graham Paige Company buying Madison Square Garden from James Norris and Arthur Wirtz in 1959. As the head barrister handling the purchase, Jennings became indoctrinated into the world of hockey, a game he didn't start following until he became an adult.

When New York Rangers president General John Reed Kilpatrick died in 1960, admiral John J. Bergen took over and enlisted Jennings to become more active with the team, not just the legal documents concerning the facility. After the 1961-62 season, the Garden Corp changed the superstructure of the team, electing Bergen to chairman of the board and naming Jennings, 41, president.

Prior to Jennings coming aboard, the flagging Rangers had missed the playoffs 14 of the previous 20 seasons, a sorry fact made even worse when you consider that four of the six teams at the time made the post-season. Jennings brought former goalie-turned coach Emile Francis on board as GM in 1964, and the franchise's fortunes started to turn. The Rangers became relevant in New York again. Their winning record in 1966-67 was their first in nine seasons. "I never went for that bunk that the Rangers had a small, hardcore clientele," Jennings told *The Hockey News* in 1967. "Hockey is and has been very popular around New York for a long time. Now that we are not finishing fifth and sixth, the fans are more vocal. Heck, I have been a rooter for 22 years – and I think that hockey is the best spectator sport of all."

Jennings arrived as a builder, but the work he did was only a trickle compared to the torrent he unleashed over the next few years. He was the point guard behind the league's six-team expansion in 1967. Jennings, with the help of the NHL's expansion committee and president Clarence Campbell, engineered the first expansion of the league, from six to 12 teams. His motives were simple, wrote Norman MacLean in *The Hockey News* at the time: "He wanted hockey to be truly major in scope – and to get in on some of the television money which football was lapping up. He talked his (NHL) lodge brothers into expansion."

Jennings helped spearhead hockey's first U.S. TV deal with CBS and was also behind the contract with NBC that decade. He was responsible for the league opening an office

in New York and hiring a public relations director in the U.S. He was also chairman of the NHL's board of governors from 1968 to 1970. Jennings was awarded the Lester Patrick Trophy in 1977 for his outstanding contribution to hockey in the U.S., and he was inducted into the Hall of Fame in 1975.

By the time Jennings, a voracious smoker, died of throat cancer at 60 in 1981, the number of U.S.-based NHL teams had grown from four to 14. He died a hockey man through and through. "I don't think he knew the first thing about hockey when the Rangers thing fell in his lap," Francis said in 2010. "But it wasn't long before he was pulling a lot of strings behind the scenes in the league. He was the driving force behind expansion. He was very ambitious and very driven."

With the NHL adopting a new goaltending award in the 1981-82 season and redefining the criteria of the Vezina Trophy, the next question was naming the hardware given to the stopper(s) allowing the fewest goals. Hockey followers predicted it would be called the Jacques Plante Trophy. Over 20 years had passed since Plante revolutionized the game by creating a goalie mask, and in 1981 he was six years retired from the game. What better way to honor this living legend than to name a goaltending award after Plante, a man who allowed few goals.

But the NHL's governors instead turned to Jennings, a man of many goals. "It made sense to honor his many contributions to the game by naming the new trophy after him," said Harry Sinden, a Hall of Fame inductee as a builder. "And that's what we did."

– By Brian Costello

 # KEN DRYDEN

KEN DRYDEN IS one of the few players who has been just as important to the game following his retirement as he was when he played it.

Dryden appeared in just six regular season games with the Montreal Canadiens in the 1970-71 season, when he became the backbone of the Habs' Stanley Cup run. He won five more Cups in his eight NHL seasons and five Vezina Trophies as the league's best goalie before retiring at 31.

Dryden has always been known as a thoughtful guy, and after retiring he embarked on a peripatetic career as a thinker. Early in his career, he left the Canadiens to complete his law degree when contract talks

in 1973 with GM Sam Pollock couldn't be settled.

In 1983, he wrote the first book on hockey that was considered literary. *The Game* has been called the best hockey book written in the English language, and it still stands more than 30 years later. His ground-breaking 1990 television series *Home Game*, based on another book, which he co-wrote with Roy MacGregor, was the first examination of hockey as culture, especially Canadian culture.

Dryden was pivotal in the formation of the Open Ice Summit in 1999, regarding the development of Canadian hockey players. Across the country, he lectures on concus-

sions, player safety and changes that need to be made to the game. He wants these conversations to continue growing. Dryden once said that hockey needs the "next forward pass" – that is, another move to revolutionize the game.

Dryden knows how to make a point, as demonstrated by his op-ed pieces for *The Toronto Star* and *The Globe and Mail*. When writers seek someone to speak intelligently about hockey, Dryden's name always comes to mind.

– By Alan Adams

43 DOUG HARVEY

SCOTTY BOWMAN, THE ultimate appraiser of hockey talent, called Doug Harvey the best defensemen he ever saw. And that included Bobby Orr. But Bowman wasn't alone in his assessment. Toe Blake, who coached Harvey and the Montreal Canadiens for six years, said he did everything well and called Harvey "the greatest defenseman who ever played hockey – bar none."

Unlike Orr, who played for only 12 years, Harvey stood the test of time. After being traded to the New York Rangers in 1961, he became player-coach and led the Blueshirts to the playoffs for the first time in four years. Not only that, but he also won the Norris Trophy and was named to the first all-star team. Part of Harvey's persona was a touch of whimsy, which he infected his teammates with wherever he played. Maurice Richard once said, "Doug had a terrific sense of humor, and he'd relax us with a gag whenever we were tense."

Harvey also played the point – along with Bernie Geoffrion – on what is considered the best power play of all time. Thanks to Harvey's uncannily accurate passes, the Canadiens created what was known as "firewagon hockey" on their way to winning a record five straight Stanley Cups from 1956 through 1960, complementing Harvey's first in 1953.

Even after retiring as a player, Harvey made news. When the rival WHA made its professional debut in the early 1970s, a bitter scramble for talent ensued. One of the prize prospects was Mark Howe, son of Gordie. The NHL bosses expected that Mark would sign with one of their teams, either Boston or Detroit. Harvey, assistant GM of the WHA's Houston Aeros, persuaded the Texas-based club to sign both Mark and his older brother Marty in 1973. The Aeros agreed and included Gordie in the package, thereby completing one of the most astonishing coups in sports.

– By Stan Fischler

44 RALPH MELLANBY

THE NEXT TIME you watch an NHL game on television, thank legendary producer Ralph Mellanby for making it as informative and entertaining as possible, Don Cherry included.

For nearly two decades, Mellanby was the executive producer of *Hockey Night in Canada.* His tenure saw 20 innovations to *HNIC*, including new technologies and modernized television coverage. "There is no question Ralph has had an impact," said former *HNIC* producer John Shannon. "His impact on how the game is covered is there, no question. Ralph brought storytelling to the game. He brought color commentators to the game, using former players to tell their stories about what it was like to play the game."

Rather than just airing the game, Mellanby was the first hockey producer who delivered layers of information, including replays, statistics and graphics. He decided not to rely solely on the game for entertainment. If the game was bad, it was his team's job to entertain. "He'd say, 'We can't be responsible for the quality of play, but we can be responsible for the quality of the intermission,'" Shannon said. "If you had a bad game, Ralph's intermissions were good so people would stay and watch. He understood entertainment."

Mellanby introduced both Howie Meeker and Cherry to a nationwide audience. Although Mellanby is the man who invented *Coach's Corner* with Cherry, he probably never envisioned how popular 'Grapes' would become. But Mellanby took the risk.

Mellanby's impact extends outside *HNIC* as well. He worked 13 Olympics and won five Emmy Awards for his coverage.

– By Alan Adams

45 DON MEEHAN

ON HIS 50TH birthday, agent Don Meehan chartered an airplane and flew over 100 of his hockey friends to Ireland for a celebratory golf outing, all at his own expense. He hosted coaches like Scotty Bowman, team executives like former Philadelphia GM Bob Clarke and president Ron Ryan, and broadcasters like Ron MacLean and Harry Neale. It was a testament to Meehan's strong connections in all segments of the hockey community.

If great teams are built through the draft, Meehan proved that a powerful sports agent can travel that same path. Meehan was the founder and president of Newport Sports, the largest and most successful hockey agency of the past three decades, and his approach from the outset was to identify top amateurs and represent them before they turned professional. The formula succeeded in 1983 when a young Pat LaFontaine was selected third overall and again two years later when Wendel Clark became a first-over-all pick.

Hailing from working-class Verdun, Que., Meehan graduated with a law degree from McGill University and went on to build a steady stable of about 125 players that included numerous stars, from Nicklas Lid-strom to P.K. Subban. By understanding both the marketplace and the concerns of those across the table from him, he negotiated shrewdly but fairly and earned the trust and friendship of players and management alike.

Meehan also branched out to represent coaches and broadcasters, as well as the NHL's on-ice officials, in their collective bargaining talks with the league. He even leveraged his extensive friendships in the game to help some secure management positions.

In the early 1990s, he was among those considered to lead the NHLPA after Alan Eagleson, but he preferred to focus on his agency. In 2015, *Forbes Magazine* ranked Newport Sports as the ninth-most valuable sports agency in the world.

– By Stu Hackel

46 IGOR LARIONOV

NO PLAYER EVER dared to challenge the authority of legendary Soviet coach Viktor Tikhonov – until Igor Larionov wrote an open letter that was published in the Russian magazine *Ogonyok* in 1988.

In the letter, Larionov was critical of Tikhonov for insisting that its players, and those of the Central Red Army club he also coached, stay in military-like barracks away from their families. Larionov also complained about the State Sports Committee's refusal to allow players to leave the country and play in the NHL. In response – proving why he often went so unchallenged – Tikhonov suspended Larionov from the army club, and he wasn't allowed to travel for a year.

However, longtime national team captain Slava Fetisov came to Larionov's defense, saying he'd no longer play under such conditions, threatening the nation's success in future world competitions. In the end, Soviet officials relented, declaring certain veteran players free to go to the NHL if they agreed to play for their country one last time at the 1989 World Championship in Sweden.

Larionov signed with Vancouver and played 14 seasons in the NHL, mostly with Detroit, where he won three Stanley Cups with the Red Wings. His courage paved the way for the exodus of several Soviet stars to North America.

Larionov learned English in Russian schools, and was so proficient in it as a youth that he soon was teaching it, earning the nickname 'The Professor.'

Larionov was inducted into the Hall of Fame in 2008. Today, he works as a player agent.

– By Denis Gibbons

FRANK CALDER

AFTER FRANK CALDER passed away on Feb. 4, 1943, the *Montreal Gazette* eulogized him as "Mr. Hockey." Tommy Gorman, who at the time was the last man living from the NHL's formative meetings in 1917, said, "The game couldn't have had a better president."

Calder came to Canada from England as a young man. Active in many sports, he was a teacher at a Montreal private school before becoming a sportswriter and then an editor at various newspapers. Calder was named secretary-treasurer of the National Hockey Association in 1914 and had a leading role in the meetings that saw the NHA rebranded as the NHL. In the early years, he quietly held the league together as teams came and went. He kept the disparate interests of the owners and governors focused when the league flourished during the Roaring Twenties and when it suffered during The Great Depression. In 1939, Calder announced that the league would carry on as normally as possible after the outbreak of the Second World War.

Calder began presenting a trophy to the NHL's top rookie in 1937. When he died after 26 years in office, the NHL renamed it the Calder Memorial Trophy.

– By Eric Zweig

BRUCE MCNALL

NOT EVERYONE CAN turn ancient coin collecting into a lucrative business, but former Los Angeles Kings owner Bruce McNall did. He turned interests in horse racing, sports and movies into successful ventures, earning him millions and proving that he was a master of all things business – at least for a little while, until the multimillionaire was found guilty of defrauding financial institutions and sentenced to almost six years in prison.

Despite McNall's trouble with the law, there's no denying his impact on the game and its players. After becoming sole owner of the Kings in 1988, he managed to pull off the unthinkable: acquire Wayne Gretzky.

Everything changed for the Kings as The Great One quickly turned L.A. into a hockey town. In the 1991-92 season, the Kings became the first California-based team in Los Angeles sports history to sell out every home game. They won their first division ti-

tle in franchise history the season prior and advanced to the Stanley Cup final for the first time in 1993. By acquiring one player, McNall singlehandedly grew the popularity of a sport in a non-traditional market.

McNall wasn't done, though. He served as chairman of the NHL's board of governors from 1992 to 1994. In that timespan, he continued to grow the sport in the U.S., introducing three new American teams: the Tampa Bay Lightning, Anaheim Mighty Ducks and Florida Panthers.

Bringing in Gretzky not only changed hockey in the U.S., it also created a trickle-down effect on the players. McNall made Gretzky the highest-paid player in the NHL at the time, prompting a significant increase in NHL player salaries, an effect still felt today.

– By Christopher Ciligot

NOT MUCH HAPPENS in the CHL without David Branch's approval.

When the Flint Firebirds fired coaches under questionable circumstances during the 2015-16 season – twice – and damaged the OHL's reputation, Branch was immediately on scene. The 68-year-old was in contact with the players, including captain Alex

Peters, who became his liaison. Branch levied an indefinite suspension for owner Rolf Nilsen. Peters said it was clear that Branch worked to keep the players' best interests in mind.

This isn't the first time, nor will it be the last, that Branch has had to step into a national story in the hockey world. He has served as the OHL commissioner since 1979 and was named CHL president in 1996. Under his reign, the OHL has grown from 12 teams to 20, and the league's television exposure has significantly increased.

He's developed a reputation as a strict disciplinarian who's levied heavy suspensions and worked to promote safety in the game on and off the ice. Branch handed out 20-game suspensions to Todd Bertuzzi in 1992 and Zack Kassian in 2010, and he suspended former Windsor Spitfires coach-GM Moe Mantha an entire season for a hazing incident in 2005.

Intentional or not, Branch is helping to remove fighting from hockey. In 2012, the OHL introduced rules punishing players who fought more than 10 times in a season, a knock against the value of enforcers. He also implemented more fighting sanctions in 2014: an automatic game misconduct for fighting immediately after any faceoff, an automatic one-game suspension for three game misconducts and an automatic one-game suspension for fighting twice in one game.

– By Sean Shapiro

50 FATHER DAVID BAUER

IN THE 1960S, NHL teams could sign players as young as 16 and farm them through a vast network of junior and minor professional teams. Father David Bauer, however, believed that athletics and education could go hand in hand. But because his Canadian national team program gave players an alternative to turning pro at such a young age, he wasn't popular with the NHL establishment.

Bauer's philosophy influenced more than amateur and international hockey. His ideals led Canadian junior hockey to value players'

education more and helped make American college hockey a viable route to the NHL.

The brother of Boston Bruins star Bobby Bauer, David Bauer was an important player at St. Michael's College and helped the Oshawa Generals win the Memorial Cup while on loan in 1944. After a brief stint in the Canadian military, Bauer began studying for the priesthood in 1946 and was ordained in 1953. He then returned to St. Michael's as a teacher and hockey coach and guided the Majors to the Memorial Cup in 1961.

After attending the World Championship in 1962, Bauer presented his idea for a national team program to the Canadian Amateur Hockey Association. He was coach or GM, or both, of the national team from 1964 to 1969 and was named to the Order of Canada in 1967. Still, most fans perceived his team as a failure because of the lack of gold medals. It wasn't until the 1972 Summit Series that Canadian fans began to appreciate how good the Soviets and other European teams were.

Canada withdrew from international hockey in 1970 after the IIHF banned Canadian professionals, and Bauer began to share his knowledge with other hockey-playing nations. When Canada returned to the Olympics in 1980, Bauer served as the team's managing director. He was named vice-president of Hockey Canada and chairman of Canada's Olympic hockey program in 1981.

Bauer passed away in 1988 at 64, before his induction into the Hockey Hall of Fame in 1989 and the IIHF Hall of Fame in 1997.

– By Eric Zweig

51 FRANK BOUCHER

FRANK BOUCHER CAPITALIZED on increasingly liberal forward passing rules to become a great playmaker on the New York Rangers' top line with brothers Bill and Bun Cook. Combining skill and sportsmanship, Boucher was given the original Lady Byng Trophy to keep after winning the award seven times in eight years from 1928 to 1935. He won the Stanley Cup as a player with the Rangers in 1928 and 1933, and then as their coach in 1940. He was the team's GM from 1949 to 1955.

During his time with the Rangers, Boucher spent 15 seasons as chairman of the NHL's rules committee. His most influential innovation was the introduction of the center ice red line for the 1943-44 season. Before the red line, NHL rules didn't allow passing from one zone to another. Instead, players carried the puck out of their own end. The red line rule allowed players to pass the puck out of their zone, as long as those passes didn't cross center ice. The modern stretch pass was still years away, but the introduction of the red line increased the speed of the game tremendously.

– By Eric Zweig

52 FRED SHERO

BOB KELLY SCORED the Stanley Cup-winning goal in Game 6 of the 1975 final, but that didn't obstruct Fred Shero from directing his sharp wit toward him. Shero tried delivering an analogy one morning while addressing the Broad Street Bullies. "Kelly," he said, "hockey is kind of like eggs and bacon for breakfast. The chicken makes a contribution,

FRANK BOUCHER

FRED SHERO

but the pig, well, he makes a sacrifice. So what are you, Kelly? A chicken or a pig?"

The room erupted in laughter as Kelly blushed. Shero had his audience in the palm of his hand.

That's how it was with 'Freddy the Fog.' Never a dull moment, never a day in which you could predict what words would tumble from the face trademarked with a mustache and glasses. And that's why the Flyers were so inspired when playing for their coach.

Shero was ahead of his time. He pioneered the use of videotape, introduced the morning skate and travelled as far as Russia to learn new strategies He was unanimously loved by his players, and he knew how to connect with them – even by making allusions to farm animals.

– By Wayne Fish

53 ROGER NEILSON

AS A MINOR baseball manager for two decades, Neilson loved flashing signs, stealing bases and playing the old hidden ball trick. Reviewing his Ontario Hockey Association and NHL resumes tells you that when Neilson moved into hockey, he brought his tricks with him.

As the grandfather of advanced statistics, Neilson revolutionized standards and analyses taken for granted today. 'Captain Video' borrowed equipment from his days as a teacher to show his team previous games, point out flaws and track tendencies. Of course, this is the standard today, but it was peculiar, to say the least, 50 years ago. Neilson was interested in tracking stats like faceoff wins and losses, scoring chances for and against, power plays

and penalty kills. He even tracked time on ice and awarded his players for hits. The NHL of today records far more advanced stats, but Neilson led the charge to track more than just goals, assists and points.

And the trap. How can you forget the trap? Although Jacques Lemaire popularized the system forcing teams in possession to dump the puck, Neilson used it in the early 1990s with the New York Rangers. He once said of his junior team, "Usually, the duller we get, the better we get."

Training camps? That was Neilson. Matching lines? Also Neilson. The coaches of the present day owe to a lot to the mysterious man who coached exactly 1,000 NHL games.

The NHL owes him, too. Through his creativity, Neilson ensured that referees and officials were always on their toes. If the goalie was pulled, he made sure they left their stick in the crease. If there was a penalty shot, he put a defenseman in net to come out and attack. If his team was shorthanded 5-on-3, he put out extra players, knowing he wouldn't be penalized.

So what followed Neilson's NHL coaching career? Plenty of rule changes, just to keep up with those tricks.

– By Matthew Stamper

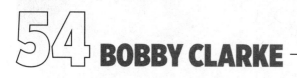

BOBBY CLARKE

ON ONE PLAY he lowered his stick, on another he raised it.

The two actions defined the Hall of Fame career of Bobby Clarke, widely regarded as one of hockey's greatest leaders. Both changed hockey history.

Many believe his questionable two-handed stick slash of Valeri Kharlamov's ankle in Game 6 changed the course of the 1972 Summit Series between Canada and the Soviet Union. Kharlamov was "killing" the Canadian crew when assistant coach John Ferguson supposedly instructed Clarke to perform the infamous deed. Clarke, already known as a win-at-all-costs player, obliged, and Kharlamov suffered a broken ankle and wasn't seen again. Canada went on to win the series.

The Philadelphia captain who was born in a small Manitoban community didn't recall Ferguson's order, but said, "If I hadn't learned to lay on a two-hander once in a while, I'd never have left Flin Flon."

Fast-forward two years to May 9, 1974, Boston Garden, Game 2 of the Stanley Cup final between the Flyers and the Bruins. The Flyers entered the game 1-17-2 in 20 games played at Boston Garden. In overtime, Clarke scored, jumped three feet off the ice and raised his stick. The curse was over. The Flyers would become the first expansion team to win a Stanley Cup.

Every career has its lows and highs. For Clarke, the contrast of those two moments in time was like no other.

– By Wayne Fish

GLEN SATHER

HE HAD JUST 80 goals and 193 points in 658 career games as an NHL left winger, but Glen Sather's success off the ice proved that he had one of the best hockey senses in the game.

Sather played an important role in Oilers history, purchasing the contract of 17-year-old phenom Wayne Gretzky from the Indianapolis Racers. But Gretzky wasn't the only franchise player Sather brought in.

BOBBY CLARKE

GLEN SATHER

Legendary names like Mike Gartner, Rick Vaive, Ray Bourque and, of course, Mark Messier filled the 1979 draft. Messier was passed by every team until the third round when Sather, then coach and vice-president of hockey operations, snatched another franchise cornerstone. Mark Spector's book *The Battle of Alberta* recounted the chief scout Barry Fraser's fight with Sather. "He wanted Messier in the third round and I wanted to wait one more," Fraser said. "I mean, he'd only scored one goal the year before...and it was one that hit him on the ass and went in, as I remember."

Sather became coach-GM in 1980, and between 1980 and 1983, he bolstered his team at every position through draft, adding defensemen Paul Coffey and Jeff Beukeboom, forwards Jari Kurri and Esa Tikkanen, and Vezina Trophy-winning goaltender Grant Fuhr. His efforts behind the bench turned an expansion franchise into a dynasty with a heavy trophy case, finishing with a coaching record of 464-268-110 in 842 games over 11 seasons (or 497-307-128 in 932 games over 13 seasons including his time with New York Rangers). 'Slats' led his Oilers team to four Stanley Cups in five seasons from 1983 to 1988. He added one more Cup in 1990 as GM, without the services of Gretzky.

At the international level, Sather led Canada to the 1984 Canada Cup. In 1994, he was the GM behind Canada's first World Championship team since 1961. In 1997, Sather was inducted into the Hall of Fame as a builder.

– By Michael Fletcher

56 PAUL HENDERSON

HE RECORDED SEVEN 20-goal seasons as an NHLer, and he played twice in the All-Star Game. But he'll forever be known for scoring one goal – the most important tally in Canadian hockey history, perhaps in the history of the game.

When Henderson flipped the puck past Vladislav Tretiak with 34 seconds left to play in Game 8 on Sept. 28, 1972, it gave Canada a 6-5 win over the Soviet Union and a 4-3-1 triumph in their epic Summit Series. He'll be forever remembered for that goal, and not a day goes by when someone doesn't ask Henderson about it. "It continues to amaze me, the mystique of 1972," Henderson said. "The

Cold War was on, the communists were using sport as propaganda, winning the Olympics and World Championships every year, and we were tired of it. If anything can bind Canada together, it's hockey. The country got caught up in it, and I've been riding the wave for 44 years."

Henderson discovered that not everyone viewed him as a hero. He and his wife Eleanor were flying from Prague to Moscow when a Russian passenger hollered his name. "That's Paul Henderson," the man said in a scolding tone. "He's a bad man. He scored that goal in 1972."

– By Bob Duff

 RENE FASEL

WHEN EUROPEAN NATIONS and the U.S. were clamoring for the inclusion of NHL players in the Olympics, Hockey Canada opposed the idea at first, preferring to reserve the competition for amateur players. It was ironic, since 26 years earlier the Canadian Amateur Hockey Association, Hockey Canada's forerunner, was putting the heat on the IIHF to allow professionals in the World Championship, while the Europeans were against it.

In 1995, Rene Fasel, a Swiss dentist and president of the IIHF, led the IIHF's negotiating team in discussions resulting in the appearance of NHL players in the Olympics for the first time in Nagano, Japan, in 1998. Fans had been deprived of NHL hockey for most of the 1994-95 season because of a lockout. When the league and NHLPA finally signed a new collective bargaining agreement, there was a commitment by both parties to go to Nagano. Fasel viewed this as an important event in giving hockey worldwide exposure. Eventually, the NHL shut down for 17 days for the Nagano Games in February 1998.

Fasel was also involved in making the decision to have a women's competition in the Olympics for the first time that same year. A World Championship had been launched in 1990, and there are now women's national teams in every continent of the world. Inline hockey has become part of the IIHF program during Fasel's presidency, too, and the Champions Hockey League was formed in Europe in 2014.

Fasel was elected president of the Swiss Ice Hockey Federation in 1985 and succeed-

ed Gunther Sabetzki as IIHF president in 1994. In 1995, he became hockey's first-ever representative on the International Olympic Committee. He also served as chairman of the 2010 Vancouver Olympics Coordination Committee.

– By Denis Gibbons

58 DOMINIK HASEK

THE IMAGE IS more than two decades old, but it's burned into Mitch Korn's brain: a 6-foot-1, 166-pound man wearing nothing but a tank top, tighty-whitey underwear, black knee socks and dress shoes. "I can remember that vision, and it's not a good one," Korn said with a laugh.

It was 1992, and Korn was the Buffalo Sabres' goaltending coach. The scantily clad newcomer staring back at him was Dominik Hasek. Korn didn't know it yet, but that was just Dom being Dom. Korn grew to expect nothing less from one of the quirkiest, most innovative, most dominant goaltenders in hockey history.

Hasek's narrative never followed a straight line. He zigged when others zagged, whether it concerned his fashion sense, his pre-game rituals, his practice habits or, most prominently, his acrobatic puckstopping style. Even his path to the NHL was circuitous.

Hasek was drafted out of his native Czechoslovakia during the Iron Curtain era, when NHL teams hesitated to select players from communist countries, worrying that they would never make the trek across the Atlantic Ocean. The Chicago Black Hawks picked Hasek 199th overall in 1983. Several months passed before he even became aware that he had been drafted. He spent most of his twenties dominating the Czech Extraliga before arriving in North America for the 1990-91 season.

That's when Korn first laid eyes on him, a couple years before they formally met. Korn, not yet working in the NHL, was attending an International League Indianapolis Ice game to watch an old pupil. He noticed Hasek, the Ice's backup goaltender, skating around the ice by himself during intermission wearing no upper padding, no gloves, no mask – just a towel around his neck. "He had his hands behind his back, and he kind of speed-skated around the rink," Korn said. "I remember seeing that and saying to myself, 'That's different.'"

Hasek was as different as they come. The hockey world just didn't know it yet. He was an obscure name even when he reached the NHL, backing up eventual Hall of Famer Ed Belfour on a powerhouse Blackhawks club that reached the 1992 Stanley Cup final. The Hawks traded Hasek to the Sabres for Stephane Beauregard and a fourth-round pick before the 1992-93 season. Hasek joined a new goaltending battery with another future Hall of Famer, Grant Fuhr. Hasek was nothing Fuhr or Korn had ever seen, with an unorthodox, desperate, floppy technique.

"It was kind of a stop, drop and roll," Fuhr said. "He did whatever he could to get himself in front of the puck. It didn't always have to be technically sound. It just had to work."

The athletic Hasek scrambled around the crease, contorted his body and made snow angels to stop pucks. He barrel-rolled and used the back of his trapper to block the goal line after being beaten on dekes. And, of course, he dropped his goal stick – his signature move. Hasek wanted the puck and knew he could retrieve it with his blocker hand if he dropped his stick. Though it worked, Korn was worried that Hasek would break his fingers, so the two came to a compromise. Their agreement: the puck needed to be on Hasek's right side and easily within reach, and he had to yank his hand away as soon he held the puck. "Imagine playing goal is a 1,000-piece jigsaw puzzle," Korn said. "Some goalies have 800 pieces, some guys have all 1,000 pieces. Rarely are all the pieces put together, and not every piece is in color. Some are in black and white. Dom had all 1,000 pieces, and his 1,000 pieces had no order. They were all scattered around that table. My job, I felt, was to give it order, to put all that stuff together to make it work so the right thing happened at the right time."

But it almost didn't for Buffalo. During the 1993 expansion draft, they protected Fuhr, not Hasek, ignoring Korn's suggestion. "I said, 'This guy can play, but you just have to have a strong stomach to watch him,' " Korn said.

No team claimed Hasek. He remained a Sabre when the 1993-94 season arrived, and suddenly the puzzle pieces fused beautifully. 'The Dominator' was born, and the most overpowering stretch of excellence by any goalie in NHL history began. He won five Vezina Trophies in the next six years. He won the Hart Trophy as league MVP and the Ted Lindsay Award (then the Lester B. Pearson) for MVP, as voted by the players in 1996-97 and 1997-98. Hasek's .930 save percentage in 1993-94 obliterated the previous record of .914. He topped his own mark three more times and held it until 2010-11, when Tim Thomas bested it. Along with running laps around the NHL, Hasek carried the Czech Republic to gold at the 1998 Olympics. His goals-against average? 0.97. His save percentage? .961.

Hasek maintained that dominance because he was so driven, not just during games but in every practice. Hasek's practice habits pushed him and Fuhr and helped their skaters become better goal scorers, since they consistently faced Hasek's best. He drilled himself on game situations and repeated new movements until he achieved perfection. "He hated to be scored on any day," Fuhr said. "The drill was staying until he got it the way he wanted it. When he got the results he wanted, then the drill could end."

Hasek finished with six Vezinas in his career. The only goaltender with more is Jacques Plante, who had seven and won six of those playing in a league with six teams and six starting goaltenders. The NHL had 26 teams when Hasek won his first Vezina and 30 when he earned his last. Plante won all his Vezinas when the trophy was awarded to the starting goalie of the team with the lowest GAA, so Hasek has the most Vezinas under the newer, more challenging system in which GMs vote on the league's best goalie.

'The Dominator' can never be replicated, but he invented a style many netminders have emulated. He gave hope to those relying on athleticism and sheer willpower over pretty technique. Elements of Hasek's scrambling style can be seen today in Jonathan Quick's play.

Hasek sits atop the list of the game's most innovative goalies, but what about the best goalies *period*? Consider that Hasek didn't become a starter until 28. If standard-setters Patrick Roy and Martin Brodeur had commenced their careers at the same age, the results would be close. Roy: 2 Cups, 326 wins. Brodeur: 1 Cup, 444 wins. Hasek: 2 Cups, 365 wins.

Hasek stands shoulder-to-shoulder with the elite. He has as strong a claim as any to the unofficial throne of goaltending's great-

est ever. "While the career may not have been as long as Patrick's or Marty's, or set the kind of records that Marty set, at the end of the day I think Dominik Hasek was the best of all time," Korn said. "And the reason is, on most of his great seasons, he didn't have teams at the level Patrick had in Montreal or Colorado and what Marty had in New Jersey. With the teams he had, Dom made way more of a difference night by night consistently to make him, for me, the best guy who has ever played."

– By Matt Larkin

LOU LAMORIELLO

LOU LAMORIELLO AND David Poile are two of the NHL's most experienced GMs. You'd think they'd have done a fair amount of business together in three decades running teams, but they've made just one deal: a 2010 swap sending center Jason Arnott from Poile's Nashville Predators to the New Jersey Devils franchise Lamoriello guided to three Stanley Cups in 28 years. "That's Lou – there was never any dancing around a deal," Poile says. "He's as straightforward and to the point as they come."

In carving a Hall of Fame career, the 75-year-old Lamoriello became famous for that candid and straightforward approach. He and his players held an old-school mentality that put the team above all else, and he owed his relentless work ethic to that philosophy.

Lamoriello's actions immediately after the Devils beat the Stars in Dallas in Game 6 of the 2000 Stanley Cup final best exemplified

that focus. He celebrated for a few hours, but the next morning on the team's charter flight to New Jersey he was back on the job, hurrying his players to board the plane and the pilots to pick things up. "He'd won a Stanley Cup with us, and less than a day later he shifted his attention to doing whatever he could to win us the Cup the next year," said former Devils center Bobby Holik. "He's all business."

– By Adam Proteau

60 FRANCOIS ALLAIRE

WHEN YOU WATCH an NHL goalie in the modern era, you're watching a goaltending style Francois Allaire helped hone. The 58-year-old never tended net at any notable level of the game, but for nearly 30 years, Allaire's impact on the best goaltenders on the planet has been immeasurable.

After starting in the QMJHL in 1983, Allaire jumped to the Montreal Canadiens organization in 1985 to become the team's first full-time goalie coach. There, he mentored a youngster named Patrick Roy, who went on to win two Stanley Cups, three Vezina Trophies and two Conn Smythe Trophies under Allaire's tutelage.

But Allaire didn't piggyback on Roy's stunning successes. As he proved when he left the Habs in the mid-1990s, his approach to stopping pucks, which centered on stellar body positioning and the butterfly, was something that could be transferred to any other netminder. Indeed, in Allaire's first year with a new NHL team – the Anaheim Ducks – he worked with goalie Guy Hebert, and the duo helped the organization to its first playoff appearance in 1997. Then he took Jean-Sebastien Giguere under his wing and steered him to a Conn Smythe Trophy in 2003 and a Stanley Cup victory in 2007. Since then, he followed a three-year stint in Toronto with a move to Colorado.

In all, Allaire's methods are world-renowned and remain highly sought-after – the best testament to his work and legacy.

– By Adam Proteau

61 WILLIE O'REE

HE IS CALLED the 'Jackie Robinson of Hockey.' A decade after Robinson broke the color barrier in baseball, Willie O'Ree was called up to play for the Boston Bruins against the Montreal Canadiens at the Montreal Forum. Jan. 18, 1958, was also the night that the prime minister of Laos, Prince Souvanna Phouma, attended the game while on a state visit to Canada – with plenty of CBC News cameras in tow. What they got was a bigger story: footage of O'Ree signing autographs for fans in the warmup and then jumping off the Bruins bench to make hockey history and set the stage for other young black hockey players to play the game.

O'Ree was sent back to the minor league Quebec Aces but returned to the NHL in the 1960-61 season. On Jan. 7, 1961, he was interviewed on *Hockey Night in Canada* and explained some of the challenges of playing in the NHL as a black man. He had taken vicious slashes to the face and admitted he had been subjected to racist insults and slurs in every game he played for Boston. He retaliated not with violence but by upping his game. He didn't want to fight, but he was determined to play, and he had to fight to prove it.

While in the spotlight, O'Ree neglected to mention that he was almost completely blind in his right eye due to an errant puck. If the league had known, he likely would have been prevented from playing. Remarkably, he kept the injury secret and had altered his playing style to compensate for his visual difficulties.

On the final *HNIC* regular season telecast in 1961, O'Ree scored for Boston against the Toronto Maple Leafs. It was his third goal of the season in 42 games. The next night in Boston against the visiting Chicago Black Hawks, he scored again. He was then dealt to the Montreal Canadiens, spending the rest of his career mostly in the WHL with the Los Angeles Blades and San Diego Gulls. It would be 13 more years before Mike Marson, the next black hockey player to play in the NHL, suited up for the Washington Capitals.

O'Ree was the ideal person to break the color barrier in hockey. He had skill and speed, he stood tall in the face of unnecessary abuse and he persevered despite an injury that would have sidelined most other players.

– By Paul Patskou

62 HAROLD BALLARD

CONN SMYTHE REFERRED to Harold Ballard as a "pirate," and that was before the irascible Ballard became sole owner of the Toronto Maple Leafs. Over the years, Ballard turned into a controversial, media-hungry, controlling figure. And under his watch, the Leafs suffered their worst times.

During the glory years of the 1960s, when Ballard stepped out of line in the front office, his wrist was slapped by Stafford Smythe, who oversaw hockey operations. Ballard loved making the headlines, so when he sold star player Frank Mahovlich to Chicago for $1 million, he did so without any authorization. When Stafford Smythe passed away, Ballard gained complete control and unceremoniously ran the team from a jail cell, having been convicted of fraud. In typical Ballard fashion, he created a media firestorm when he claimed that his jail resembled a hotel.

As the team became worse on the ice, Ballard became more unpredictable. His most outrageous stunt was firing coach Roger Neilson and then rehiring him – but not before insisting that he appear behind the bench with a paper bag over his head.

The Leafs achieved little on-ice success during Ballard's nearly two decades as majority owner, but the years were never dull.

– By Paul Patskou

 **STAN MIKITA**

LIKE MANY INGENIOUS ideas, Stan Mikita's revolutionary discovery that forever changed the game of hockey was an accident.

Mikita, who spent his entire 22-year professional career with the Chicago Black Hawks, is credited with popularizing the curved stick. As legend has it, one day Mikita's stick caught in the doorway leading onto the ice at practice. When he pulled it out, he saw an L shape in the blade. Instead of retrieving a new one, an angry Mikita slammed a puck against the boards. He liked the sound and the feel of the shot, so he tried a few more wristers. A couple days later, Mikita figured out ways to bend the blade without cracking it. He tried various ways of heating and contorting the stick. He would heat and then bend the blade by sticking it under a door and pulling it up.

In the following days, Mikita experimented with his sticks. He heated the blade with a blowtorch and bent the blade with his foot. To maintain the shape, he shoved the blade under a dressing room door, using books to hold it in place.

Realizing its potential, players around the league quickly adopted the curved stick, and manufacturers began producing them. By the late 1960s, the league began regulating the amount of curve players could have on their blades, mostly to protect goalies.

The curved stick may be the symbol of Mikita's legacy, but his name is littered across the NHL history books. The Slovak-born Canadian is Chicago's all-time leader in points (1,467), assists (926) and games played (1,394). He only won the Stanley Cup once, in 1961, but his list of honors is impressive: four Art Ross Trophies, two Harts and two Lady Byngs. Mikita is the only player in NHL history to win the Art Ross, Hart and Lady Byng Trophies in the same season, which he achieved twice in the 1966-67 and 1967-68 campaigns. He was inducted into the Hall of Fame in 1983 and was honored with a statue outside the United Center.

– By Alan Adams

64 MARK MESSIER

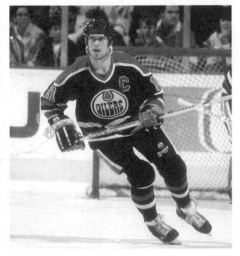

ON AUG. 9, 1988, the Edmonton Oilers, winners of four Stanley Cups in five years, altered the hockey universe by trading their fourth captain in team history, The Great One, to the Los Angeles Kings. Their fifth? Mark Messier.

The Oilers selected the native of Edmonton, Alta., and alternate captain as their new leader. Messier didn't disappoint his hometown. He weathered the loss of the best hockey player of all-time by leading his Oilers to their fifth Cup, his first of two without Wayne Gretzky, in his second season as team captain.

Messier sits near the top of most career leaderboards, ranking second in games played (1,756), eighth in goals (694), third in assists (1,193) and third in points (1,887). The best leaders take over in the big moments, and Messier shined brightly as he is tied for 14th in game-winning goals (92). And when the big moments became bigger, the light emitting off Messier must have blinded. On the playoff charts, he finished fourth in games played (236), second in goals (109), second in assists (186) and second in points (295). He joined lists featuring Ken Dryden, Frank Mahovlich and Bryan Trottier as six-time Cup-winners. He was one of only three NHL players to captain three franchises and the only one to ever captain multiple franchises to a Stanley Cup.

Messier switched teams three times in his NHL career, but the 'C' was never removed from his jersey after that Gretzky trade until his retirement in 2004. For the past 10 years, "the player who exemplifies great leadership qualities to his team, on and off the ice" is given the Mark Messier NHL Leadership Award, after its namesake selects him. In 2007, Messier was inducted into the Hall of Fame.

– By Jimmy Huynh

65 BOB NICHOLSON

WHEN AN ITEM on a person's resume is "architect of Hockey Canada," there doesn't need to be much else. Being one of the driving forces behind an institution as powerful and universally respected as Canada's hockey program is pretty much mic drop material.

So it's no secret why Bob Nicholson, a recent Order of Hockey in Canada recipient, is one of hockey's most respected voices. His run at Hockey Canada, including 16 years as president and CEO, from 1998 to 2014, was a resounding success on and off the ice, starting with three Olympic gold medals from the men and four from the women, 12 World Junior Championships, five World Championships and 10 World Women's Championships.

His work wasn't limited to superstars, however. Nicholson helped grow and, in some cases, preserve hockey at the grassroots level, keeping it safe and viable amid rising costs and changing demographics. He also helped elevate women's hockey from its little-known infancy to a sport with millions of fans and viewers in Canada.

In some ways, his tenure at Hockey Canada was the most pressure-packed job worldwide. He needed to please a country with a religious passion for the game and a fan base that would never be satisfied with anything but the best in the world. And he succeeded, helping transform Hockey Canada into a superpower both on the ice and financially. In doing so, Nicholson developed contacts all over the globe. From Boston to Jokerit, from Prince Albert to Moscow, anybody with deep ties to hockey knows and respects the work Nicholson did for Canada.

So it's no surprise that when the NHL's worst franchise desperately needed help pulling itself out of the cellar, it turned to Nicholson, who is now the CEO of Oilers Entertainment Group. Nicholson is charged with returning the Edmonton Oilers to on-ice respectability while overseeing all aspects of business and hockey operations, including the new arena district that opened in the fall of 2016.

If he can achieve for the Oilers what he achieved for Hockey Canada, Edmonton will be forever in his debt. "Bob Nicholson is an exceptional talent with a world-class reputation and deep relationships across the hockey world, from junior player development to world-scale events and large corporate sponsors," said Oilers owner Daryl Katz in the announcement. "He has been an innovator in driving new sport-based revenue models, and we feel very fortunate he has chosen to move to Edmonton and become part of our team."

– By Rob Tychkowski

BILL TORREY

# BILL TORREY

SHORTLY AFTER LEAVING his job as executive vice-president and GM of the California Golden Seals, Bill Torrey watched from afar as the last-place Seals traded for Montreal's minor-pro prospect Ernie Hicke and the Canadiens' first pick, 10th overall, in exchange for the Seals' first-overall pick. The first selection became Guy Lafleur.

It was a move Torrey would never make as GM of the New York Islanders. Craving the best picks possible, Torrey stocked his 1972 expansion team with young talent, a team-building strategy others copied.

Earlier expansion teams, seeking a quick path to competitiveness, had peddled picks for proven veterans. Not Torrey. In 1973, with Denis Potvin as the prize, Montreal GM Sam Pollock tried mightily to pry away Torrey's first-overall pick. Torrey had already traded for Potvin's older brother, Jean, as an inducement for Denis to join his club rather than be lured by the rival WHA. Pollock bargained with Torrey right up to the moment the Islanders made their selection, but

'Bowtie Bill' held firm and drafted his cornerstone defenseman for what became a Stanley Cup dynasty.

Along with scouting director Jim Devellano, Torrey drafted the bulk of his championship clubs over the next few years, including Clark Gillies, Dave Langevin, Stefan Persson, Bryan Trottier, Mike Kaszycki, Ken Morrow, Mike Bossy, John Tonelli, Steve Tambellini, Duane Sutter, Brent Sutter and Tomas Jonsson.

Torrey was also the first GM to demonstrate the value of the trade deadline deal in 1980, when he helped secure the Islanders' first Cup by shipping two high-draftee veterans, Billy Harris and Dave Lewis, to the Kings for two-way center Butch Goring.

His formidable track record with new franchises continued after his Islanders' tenure. Torrey joined the expansion Florida Panthers as president in 1993, guiding their fortunes to a Stanley Cup final in 1996 and helping spread the game in a large, non-traditional market.

– By Stu Hackel

# KEN LINSEMAN

IF YOU HATED Ken 'The Rat' Linseman when he was playing, don't read further, because one of the most agitating players the game has ever seen is doing fine post-career. Actually, he's doing great.

Linseman made a name for himself dancing near and sometimes over the line of mayhem on the ice. He now travels the world surfing with his son, hitting up Hawaii, Indonesia, his beach house in Puerto Rico and top

locations in Canada so secret they don't even have surf shops. "Hawaii and Indonesia are the best," he said. "Indonesians are sweet people."

Along with killing waves, Linseman, now 59, sharpens his mind and keeps the cash flowing by developing commercial real estate properties such as pharmacies. Not that cash was ever problematic for him. In his early NHL days, Linseman bought apartments in San Diego as investments, dabbled in junk bonds and incorporated himself to maximize his salary. "The teams were paying my company, actually," he said. "Ever since my signing bonus was taxed, I started to ask a lot of questions. My pension plan is probably five times, maybe 10 times what it would have been."

Before Linseman even arrived at The Show, he did things differently and every NHLer can thank him for his individuality. After all, it was The Rat's legal challenge against the WHA in 1977 that paved the way for 18-year-olds to play in the rebel league and forced the NHL to drop the draft age from 20. "It was time for me to turn pro," Linseman said. "Alan Eagleson came around and said there would be no underage contracts, but John Bassett thought it was a great idea."

Bassett owned the WHA's Birmingham Bulls, and one year after Linseman led his franchise in scoring, the Toronto-based owner brought in a raft of other talented teenagers, including Michel Goulet, Rob Ramage, Rick Vaive and Craig Hartsburg. By then, Linseman had moved on to the NHL's Philadelphia Flyers.

Linseman played on many talented teams in the 1980s, suiting up for the Flyers, Bruins and Oilers, and winning a Stanley Cup with Edmonton in 1984. " 'Thank God,' I thought at the time," he said. "That was my third final."

As for regrets, Linseman had a few, but one in particular comes to mind. "My first time back in Edmonton, I was standing in front of the net and Andy Moog tripped," he said. "Now, a lot of times I got called for things I didn't do, but before I knew it, my old friend Lee Fogolin was beating on me, and I think I might have bit him. But we talked after the game."

Unsurprisingly, Linseman's mix of skill (his career high was 92 points in a season) and nastiness made him an archetype, and it's gratifying for him to still be evoked today as someone to be compared to. "People bring up Brad Marchand," he said. "It's nice to see a good player who plays my style."

Based in New Hampshire, Linseman still straps on the skates for alumni games throughout the Maritimes and other charity matches, including a surfers vs. hockey players contest that saw him skate for both sides. His daughter plays hockey, as does a niece, who is currently with the University of New Hampshire. And despite his notoriety, Linseman said his interactions with fans are always positive. "I certainly hear about how much people hated me," he said. "But it's all good."

Overall, Linseman looks back fondly on his hockey days. Mark Messier, Glenn Anderson and Kevin Lowe all became his good friends, and the camaraderie he enjoyed during and after his playing career he has since employed in his business life. "Playing a sport, there's such a parallel to business," he said. "It's fun when you can pull something together with a group of people."

– By Ryan Kennedy

68 BILL MASTERTON

BILL MASTERTON WAS living the dream of playing in the NHL when tragedy struck, changing hockey forever. After years of toiling in the minors, Masterton retired in 1967 without receiving a sniff from an NHL team, but when the league doubled from six teams to 12 for the 1967-68 season, Masterton left a job in contract administration to join the Minnesota North Stars. He even scored the first goal in franchise history.

The North Stars were playing the Oakland Seals in January when Masterton made his patented move: crossing the opposing blue line and cutting to one side before passing the puck to a teammate. Oakland defensemen Larry Cahan and Ron Harris moved in to check Masterton, who fell backwards and

slammed the back of his head against the ice. With blood running from his nose and ears, the 29-year-old rookie center was rushed to the hospital. Doctors operated for over 24 hours to try to save him but were unsuccessful. He died on Jan. 15 as a result of a massive brain injury.

Masterton was the first player to die directly from injuries suffered in an NHL game. His memory lives on in the Bill Masterton Memorial Trophy, awarded annually to the NHL player who best exemplifies the qualities of perseverance, sportsmanship and dedication to hockey.

Like almost every other player in the NHL at the time of his injury, Masterton, wasn't wearing a helmet, even though he wore one at every other level of the sport. His death stirred talk of the need for head protection. But helmets in the NHL at that time were considered a sign of weakness.

Masterton's death changed that stigma.

Eleven years later, the NHL mandated using helmets. By that time, the majority of players were already wearing one. The era of helmetless players ended in 1997 when the last grandfathered holdout, Craig MacTavish, retired.

Masterton's death also underlined the need for improving the NHL's life insurance policies. Masterton left possibly $100,000 to his family, including $50,000 in life insurance that the NHL carried on each player, and a $10,000 league accident policy.

– By Alan Adams

69 FRANK ZAMBONI

THE NAME IS synonymous with the product his company builds – like Ski-Doo once was and Kleenex still is. Other companies build ice-resurfacing machines, but almost everyone calls them Zambonis.

Frank Zamboni was born in Utah in 1901 and later moved to Southern California, where the family opened a skating rink in 1939. Looking for quicker and easier ways to resurface the ice, Frank began tinkering with a tractor and sled in 1942. He built an improved version of the machine in 1947 but was still unsatisfied with the results. Two years later, Frank developed a new design that resurfaced the ice properly. He received a patent in 1953.

In 1950, Frank built a Zamboni for Sonja Henie's ice show. On New Year's Day in 1954, a Zamboni resurfaced the ice between a show and an NHL game at the Boston Garden. That same year, the Bruins bought their own Zamboni. Other teams soon followed.

Before the Zamboni, it took an hour to resurface a rink, meaning the quick cleanups during intermissions did little. A clean surface at the beginning of each period helped speed up the game. The Zamboni even provided new marketing opportunities, and as more clubs provided fans with between-period entertainment on the ice, the NHL adopted a rule in the early 1990s that required teams to use two Zambonis.

– By Eric Zweig

FRANK ZAMBONI (LEFT) WITH SON RICHARD

70 JACQUES LEMAIRE

DURING MOST OF his 17 seasons as an NHL coach, Jacques Lemaire grew accustomed to the somewhat hostile greeting he'd receive when he brought his teams to town. There would be the same newspaper stories knocking Lemaire's neutral zone trap and how it took the fun out of watching games. Players on opposing teams were interviewed on TV and the radio about how difficult it was to play against Lemaire's "shut it down" style, which they invariably suggested was ruining hockey. "When I came in, we did what we had to do," said Lemaire, who turned offens-minded players like Scott Stevens and Bobby Carpenter into committed defensive forces. "And all teams play like that."

Lemaire changed the game with his defensive style. The Montreal Canadiens had a version of the trap that some called the "left wing lock," which had been used in Europe since the 1970s, but Lemaire made it mainstream with the New Jersey Devils, who won three Stanley Cups (one under Lemaire) after adopting it. Four skaters clog the neutral zone while a forechecker forces the puck-carrier to either side of the ice and ultimately into a giveaway. When the team turns the puck over, one winger drops back and forms a three-man wall with the defensemen while the center and other winger aggressively play the puck.

Along with improving goaltenders, the trap is blamed for reducing scoring. Efforts to increase scoring are an ongoing reaction to combat Lemaire's ingenuity. "It did change the game," Lemaire said. "What we did had an impact on the game. Yes, I'm proud of it, but I'm more proud of what was accomplished by those teams."

– By Rich Chere

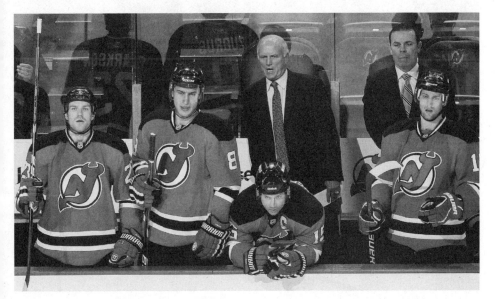

71 BUNNY AHEARNE

BUNNY AHEARNE WORE many hats: travel agent, secretary of the British Ice Hockey Federation and president of the IIHF among them. To a hockey-mad nation, however, Ahearne held one title: archenemy of Canada.

Three years after taking over in Britain, Ahearne aspired to break Canada's dominance in Olympic hockey, recruiting hockey-playing British expats from North America to play in the 1936 Winter Games and upsetting Canada to win the gold medal.

As IIHF president, Ahearne brokered a backroom deal on the final day of the 1964 Olympic tournament to change the tie-breaking formula, which cost Canada the bronze medal. He struck his final blow against Canada in 1969. Tired of losing to full-time players of the Soviet Union, Canada sought permission to bolster its lineup. In Crans, Switzerland, IIHF delegates voted that World Championship rosters could include nine minor pros or reinstated amateurs. A faction led by the Soviets grew concerned that this would taint their players, risking their Olympic eligibility. Ahearne agreed, reversing the decision. Canada withdrew from international hockey out of retribution.

– By Bob Duff

72 SIDNEY CROSBY

A NATURAL CURIOSITY lives within Sidney Crosby. History is one of his interests, but just about anything that comes up in conversation, or finds its way into his consciousness, is ripe for wondering. Luckily for the hockey world, Crosby's keen interest and thirst for detail find their apex in the sport.

Sagging ever since winning two Stanley Cups in the early 1990s, the Pittsburgh Penguins were giddy to win the draft lottery in 2005. They added Crosby, and he rewarded them by becoming his generation's best player.

At the end of the 2016-17 season, he had 382 goals and 1,027 points in 782 games, ranking sixth all-time in points per game at 1.313. In 2009, at 21 years old, he became the youngest captain in NHL history to lift the Cup. His awards case includes three Stanley Cups, two Hart Trophies, two Art Ross Trophies, three Ted Lindsay Trophies, two Conn Smythe Trophies and two Olympic golds, one of which he earned at the 2010 Vancouver Games, where he scored the overtime goal in the gold medal game.

His curiosity bug makes him wonder what his numbers might be if he had not lost significant time to injury, most notably a concussion in January 2011. He was limited to eight games over the ensuing 15 months as he endured symptoms, setbacks, various medical therapies and, from some corners, scrutiny for his extended absence.

Crosby learned a lot about the frustrating and unpredictable nature of concussions, and through his battle the sports world did, too. "It raised a lot of awareness. It was a tough thing for him to go through and his family and the organization," said Ray Shero, Pittsburgh's GM at that time whose son Chris was also battling a concussion.

It wasn't until the 2012-13 season that Crosby was fully cleared, and he had to wait until January for the season to begin because of a lockout. He was his old self again, though, putting up 56 points in 36 games. He probably would have won another NHL scoring title if not for a broken jaw late in the season that required surgery.

Shero is among those who marvel at Crosby's ability, passion and grace both on and off the ice. Once, Shero went to his office on a Sunday morning following a home game at the now-razed Mellon Arena and was spooked to hear what he thought was a mouse in the players' lounge. Then he saw a much bigger shadow. It was Crosby, who had come in to have a bowl of cereal and watch TV, even though he had perfectly comfortable living arrangements at that time on the estate of Penguins Hall of Famer and co-owner Mario Lemieux. "He's a rink rat," Shero said. "He's a great person, with what he's gone through – not just injuries but expectations and criticism."

– By Shelly Anderson

 73 PUNCH IMLACH

WHEN GEORGE 'PUNCH' Imlach arrived at Maple Leaf Gardens as Toronto's new assistant GM in 1958, he was relatively unknown. In a matter of weeks, however, he took over the coaching duties and vacant GM job. Buried in last place, he declared that his team would make the playoffs, prompting owner Conn Smythe to ask, "Did we hire a coach or a madman?"

Imlach instilled confidence in his players through the power of positive thinking and made the playoffs on the last night of the 1958-59 season. As the players came to like him, he became popular in Toronto and then respected across the league. He mixed key veterans with talented juniors to win four Stanley Cups in six seasons – the last in 1967, with an over-the-hill gang. Imlach was colorful, cocky, crude and old-school, but he was one of the most successful and respected coaches of his generation.

– By Paul Patskou

74 BRENDAN SHANAHAN

BRENDAN SHANAHAN NEVER takes the easy way out or the road most travelled. His Hall-of-Fame career includes a 21-year tenure in the NHL, an Olympic gold medal, an early post-retirement NHL job and his current role as president of the Toronto Maple Leafs.

Throughout it all, the 48-year-old Toronto native hasn't shied away from any challenge. That's earned him universal respect within the game, and his ability to use his extraordinary number of connections has helped achieve his goals.

This is one of the keys to Shanahan's rise through the hockey world: his willingness to learn from the game's best minds, to focus on a vision for success and, in the act of selling and carrying out that vision, to serve as a consensus-builder unafraid to take heat for the people and the processes he believes in.

That's why high-profile personnel are so eager to follow his lead. "I can tell you, if I want anybody recruited to go anywhere, I'm sending Brendan," said Lou Lamoriello after Shanahan hired him as Maple Leafs GM in the summer of 2015.

After Shanahan's playing career ended in 2009, he became the NHL's vice-president of hockey operations. Nearly two years later, he succeeded Colin Campbell as the league's chief disciplinarian. But whereas the old-school Campbell sent out the rulings on his suspensions and let hockey fans grumble about them, Shanahan stood before a camera after virtually every ruling and, as an expression of accountability, explained the NHL's reasoning on why it acted as it did.

That willingness to teach, to inform, to eschew a confrontational attitude in favor of one that helps those around him learn and grow – that's the Shanahan way. As a player, he wasn't above using his fists to make a point, but as a hockey gatekeeper he's evolved into a statesman and, most importantly for Leafs fans, a big-picture salesman extraordinaire who's convinced Lamoriello, coach Mike Babcock and numerous others to accompany him on a tough, lengthy franchise rebuild.

– By Adam Proteau

75 ALEX OVECHKIN

ONE YEAR BEFORE Alex Ovechkin was drafted first overall by the Washington Capitals, Florida Panthers GM Rick Dudley stepped up to the draft podium in 2003 and called his name with the 265th pick. Dudley argued that factoring in leap years, Ovechkin was eligible. While the fantastical scheme was quickly overruled, Ovechkin was a worthy target for such a ploy.

After a decade in the NHL, Ovechkin has six Richard Trophies, three Hart Trophies, and seven 50-plus-goal seasons, and he had amassed more than 500 goals. By 30, he had already settled the question of whether he is the greatest Russian player of all time. Continually hitting the 50-goal plateau in an era where the feat is increasingly rare, 'Ovie' trails only Mario Lemieux and Mike Bossy in per-game goal scoring proficiency in the modern era.

Beyond his Hall of Fame production, Ovechkin has been embraced by North American fans as no Russian before him. He shot to instant superstardom in a 52-goal, 106-point rookie year that featured 'The Goal' – an inimitable circus shot that defined his early success. He even beat out uber rookie Sidney Crosby to capture the Calder Trophy. Fans gravitated to Ovechkin's distinct flair as much as his on-ice gifts. He was the marketable electric newcomer the league needed after losing the previous season to a lockout. Children across North America began sporting yellow laces and tinted visors, charmed by the boyish enthusiasm and over-the-top celebrations of Washington's No. 8. He faced derision from conservative hockey pundits, particularly for his infamous 2009 'fire stick' celebration, but Ovechkin was undeterred by his critics. Never has

'Alex the Great' allowed outsiders to dictate his persona.

The instant he arrived in Washington, Ovechkin made every effort to endear himself to the Capitals. After his very first practice, he scribbled down teammates' names and rehearsed pronouncing them. The rookie also insisted on rooming with an English-only speaker on the road, opting for immersion rather than the familiarity offered by Russian-speaking Dainius Zubrus. By 24, Ovechkin was named the Caps' captain – a unanimous choice by teammates and at the time only the sixth Russian captain in NHL history.

While most of Ovechkin's soundbites are on the lighter side, he occasionally speaks on the game's bigger issues, and his voice echoes through the hockey world. Before the NHL committed to participate in the 2014 Sochi Olympics, Ovechkin said he'd be suiting up for Russia whether the Capitals allowed him or not. He has said the same about the 2018 Games in Pyeongchang, South Korea. If you're the NHL and your most market-able player speaks up – one who has an asteroid named after him, at that – you take note.

When negotiating his second contract, Ovechkin had two years of superstar production on his resume and was in the midst of a 65-goal season. Capitals owner Ted Leonsis had been burned before, giving out an ill-fated seven-year, $77-million contract to Jaromir Jagr. GM George McPhee, meanwhile, had only handed out one no-trade clause in his management career. But all the leverage was Ovechkin's. He was the league's hottest talent and a TV draw who sold jerseys by the bushel and brought fans to the rink. He'd previously dismissed his big-name agent Don Meehan but managed to secure the deal with only the supervision of his mother, Tatiana, and an attorney to examine the fine print. The 13-year, $124-million deal was the most lucrative in league history. Considering Ovechkin's habit of potting 50 goals year after year, and his singlehanded influence on breathing new life into the Washington hockey market, the contract may just be a bargain.

– By Casey Ippolito

76 GUNTHER SABETZKI

FED UP WITH its amateur teams losing to the Soviets and Czechoslovaks at the World Championship and Olympics, the Canadian Amateur Hockey Association withdrew from both competitions in 1970 because of the IIHF's refusal to allow professionals to participate. Canada had been scheduled to host the World Championship that year. Gunther Sabetzki, who served as the IIHF's president from 1975 to 1994, was the man who headed the successful effort leading to Canada's return.

During his presidency, the IIHF finally approved the participation of professional players in the World Championship in time for the 1976 event in Poland. The U.S. used NHL players for the first time that year, and Canada returned with a full roster the next year in Vienna. As a peace offering, the IIHF guaranteed that the World Championship wouldn't start until after the NHL regular season was over so that players not involved in the play-offs could play. On the other side of the ocean, Sabetzki exerted his influence to convince reluctant European nations to compete in the first Canada Cup tournament in 1976.

Sabetzki was one of the founding members of the German Ice Hockey Federation in 1963 and helped form the first German women's league in 1982. He became the first German elected president of the IIHF, which jumped from a membership of 31 countries to 50 under his leadership.

The president also had a warm heart for the less fortunate. Children in countries suffering hardships or torn apart by war received donations of hockey equipment under his direction. He also arranged for Anatoli Tarasov, the godfather of Soviet hockey, to travel to North Korea and China to aid in the development of hockey in those countries.

Sabetzki was elected to the Hall of Fame in 1995.

– By Denis Gibbons

77 JAROMIR JAGR

JAROMIR JAGR HAS been in the NHL longer than several teams – including his current one, the Florida Panthers. As the league's most senior member, his biggest contribution these days may be helping his much younger teammates.

When the Florida Panthers traded for Jagr before the 2015 trade deadline, Dale Tallon, president of hockey operations and then the team's GM, hoped Jagr still had gas left in the tank. But Tallon is the first to admit that he had no idea what Jagr was bringing to his Panthers. "Pavel Bure is probably the last star this organization has had, so bringing in Jaromir Jagr was a boon for the entire Florida Panthers franchise," Tallon said. "He's a star name who gave us credibility in our market. He's one of those rare guys who don't come around very often. We're very fortunate to have him."

On the day Jagr was acquired from New Jersey for draft picks, the Panthers churned

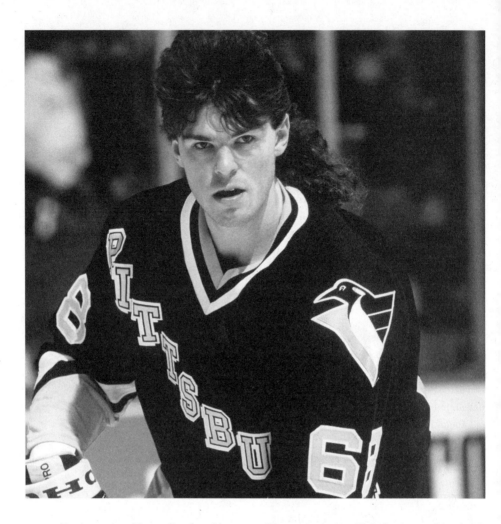

out replica jerseys and immediately sold out. Aleksander Barkov, then 19 and in his second NHL season, was so excited upon hearing about the trade that he didn't believe initial reports. Barkov called a member of the Florida coaching staff to confirm the news. When Jagr arrived a few days later, he was placed on a revamped top line with Barkov and Jonathan Huberdeau, whose combined age was still younger than Jagr's. "He brings dedication and passion, and it has helped our entire organization," Tallon said days after Jagr finished the 2015-16 season first on the team with 66 points and second with 27 goals.

"Our young guys think they're working hard, and then they see what he's doing. It draws guys in. They've made more of a commitment. It's been nothing but a positive."

In 2015-16, Jagr helped turn Florida's fortunes around. After missing the playoffs in his first run with the Panthers, he helped lead Florida to an Atlantic Division title and a playoff berth.

Elected one of four captains at the 2016 All-Star Game in Nashville, Jagr was mobbed by not only fans and media but his temporary teammates as well. An autographed jersey in what could be his final All-Star Game appearance was in popular demand by millionaire athletes, many of whom had his poster on their bedroom walls as kids. "He's the eighth wonder of the world," said teammate Vincent Trocheck, a 24-year-old who grew up in Pittsburgh. "It's crazy to think I grew up watching him, lived around the corner from him. I had a VHS highlight tape of which half belonged to Jagr. Now I'm playing with him. It's just incredible."

In his first two seasons in the NHL, Jagr sipped from the Stanley Cup with the Pitts-burgh Penguins and hasn't slowed down much since. Although he hasn't won it all since he was a shaggy-haired 20-year-old playing alongside Mario Lemieux, Jagr continues to chase the dream.

And he's already a lock for the Hall of Fame. Heading into the 2017-18 season, Jagr was fourth all-time in games played (1,711), third in goals (765), fifth in assists (1,149) and second in points (1,914).

– By George Richards

78 HOWIE MEEKER

HOWIE MEEKER DIDN'T change hockey as a player, even though he won the Calder Trophy in 1947 as a Toronto Maple Leafs right winger. He didn't change it as a coach, either, as his 1956-57 Leafs missed the playoffs. And his stint as the first active NHLer to serve in parliament was more a curious novelty than anything.

No, Meeker's legacy to hockey is that he was first to take to the national airwaves to critique and criticize the game he so loved. With his squeaky, shrill voice, boundless enthusiasm and quirky catchphrases, it was difficult to miss Meeker during his tenure as a *Hockey Night in Canada* analyst from 1969 to 1990. But it wasn't how he said it as much as the way he expressed himself that made Meeker a visionary. "Howie had a way of dissecting the game," fellow *HNIC* broadcaster Brian McFarlane told CBC.

Meeker became Canadian hockey's voice, using video replay to explain the game's nuances to the masses, becoming the first TV analyst to point out on a nightly basis the mistakes the world's best players had committed. "He revolutionized analysis of the game with his telestrator," said *HNIC's* Scott Oake.

– By Bob Duff

79 ERIC LINDROS

IT'S A BRIGHT fall day on a tree-lined street in one of Toronto's most exclusive neighborhoods, but the rich and/or famous are nowhere to be seen. Things are pleasantly quiet on this Thursday morning in mid-November. It's no more than a mile or so north of the bedlam that is downtown, but here, amid a mass of bright yellow leaves, there is nothing but calm and serenity.

On one of the houses, there's a makeshift sign from a torn cardboard box posted on the front door. In black magic marker ink, it reads: "Dear Guest: Please refrain from knocking at this time. Thank you."

The door opens and a mountain of a man stands in the doorway. His hands look as though they could swallow you whole, then crumple you up and throw you away like a piece of scrap paper. He's unshaven and graying at the temples, wearing blue sweat pants and a T-shirt with a Batman logo on the chest.

This is where the tranquility ends. Eric Lindros apologizes for the mess as he walks past three baby car seats at the door and pushes a child's toy out of the way with his foot. Two nannies are tending to nine-week-old twins, Ryan Paul and Sophie Rose. Lindros' wife, Kina, rounds out the 1-on-1 defense, running everywhere and seemingly doing everything. Resident handyman Vern is omnipresent, taking massive doors off frames and providing the man of the house a little relief from his honey-do list. Oblivious to all the commotion is George, a Hungarian waterfowl-hunting dog who is scared to death of ducks. He's licking the face of little Carl Pierre, who's displaying the kind of behavior typical of a 17-month-old child – perfectly content and squealing with joy one moment, inquisitive the next, then agitated and impatient, and eventually in full meltdown mode.

Lindros has just returned from his weekly pickup game at the Toronto arena where he first displayed his greatness more than a quarter-century ago. It was decrepit back in the 1980s, and not much has changed. "We have a real good skate every Thursday morning," Lindros says. "I had a good line this morning: Rob DiMaio and 'Kipper' (Nick Kypreos)."

There's something decidedly different about 'The Big E' these days. He speaks excitedly about how a Costco is coming soon to his neighborhood, because that means he doesn't have to trek across town anymore. He talks about how Pampers are much better than Huggies for absorbing wetness. And he suggests never buying bulk batteries at Costco because it's impossible to get through the enormous package before they die out.

Just then, Carl Pierre sits on his lap and reaches for something. Unable to determine what his son wants, Lindros says, "Use your words," before discovering Carl Pierre wants to play with a set of keys. At one point, Kina walks across the kitchen with two packages of what look like drink boxes, but they're actually pre-mixed formula with a nipple attached for use in the car during moments of desperation. They were the brainchild of a guy Kina went to university with, and he sent the couple a care package full of them.

Eric (under his breath): They're f---ing brilliant.

Kina: I'm sending them all to the women's shelters.

Eric: Those ones? Why?

Kina: Because the kids don't like them.

Eric: Well, so much for brilliant.

Somewhere along the way, Lindros became an everyman. All right, "everyman" is a relative term here. Lindros earned almost $50 million over the course of his playing career and has invested wisely. He doesn't need a regular gig and can still live in the most well-to-do area of the biggest, richest city in Canada. He has two nannies and three cars – a Lexus, Range Rover and Porsche Cayenne – in the driveway. He owns a hunting camp in Quebec and can afford to donate $5 million to the London Health Sciences Centre. Not exactly Fred Flintstone coming back from a hard day in the quarry, but there is a basic quality about Lindros these days. He's as happy and content as he's been in years, and more at peace with himself than he ever was during his brilliant but turbulent hockey career.

Perhaps that has something to do with Lindros living in the knowledge that he was right all along and those in hockey who viewed him as a petulant, selfish and spoiled superstar owe him an apology. The trail he blazed on players' rights and concussion awareness that earned him so much derision during his career have become standard procedure for today's player. There is no difference between what Nathan MacKinnon and Max Domi did orchestrating their destinations as junior players and what Lindros did almost 27 years ago when he refused to report to Sault Ste. Marie and ended up in Os-

hawa. NHL players can thank the likes of Lindros for no-trade clauses. And those who look out for their own health interests rather than keeping quiet and playing can also take inspiration from Lindros, the man who shut himself down and refused to play until he was healthy enough to do so, in spite of the avalanche of opinion against him at the time. "Listen, I wasn't perfect. No one is perfect," Lindros says. "But I do sit here and feel quite comfortable about my health going forward. I feel good. We're going to be fine. Our kids are healthy, and we're lucky. We're just tired."

***

Now 43, Lindros is a long way from the teenaged phenom who first took the hockey world by storm at the World Junior Championship in 1991. Since then, the world juniors has gathered the best teenage players in the world together during the holiday season for more than 40 years, and a tournament that was once the sole domain of hockey nerds has become a major revenue generator and marquee event. To say Lindros was the driving force behind this monolith wouldn't be a stretch. The world juniors, particularly when played in Canada, can generate approximately $60 million for Hockey Canada and its partners. And TSN, which started broadcasting the event in 1991 with Lindros its centerpiece, has found a lucrative advertising windfall at a time on the calendar when nobody has money and advertisers have maxed out their Christmas budgets.

TV producer Paul Graham masterminded the television spectacle the WJC has become today. It's the closest thing the hockey world has to March Madness. It was Graham's idea to dress it up as a major TV event, and with the hottest prospect on the planet anchoring the Canadian team in 1991, he had a player who could hold eyeballs. Organizers in host Saskatchewan guaranteed that they would deliver $1 million to Hockey Canada, a target they far exceeded. Since then, TSN has built its WJC coverage to make it a must-see event with an enduring legacy.

The audience for Canada's 3-2 win over the Soviet Union in the 1991 gold medal game – one in which little-known Newfoundlander John Slaney scored the winner with just over five minutes to go in the third period – was 1.4 million, a record for TSN at the time. Lindros was spectacular in the tournament, with six goals and 17 points, part of a three-year run that made him Canada's leading WJC scorer and one of its all-time greatest players.

Twenty-five years later, Lindros remembers the tournament well, but he never sensed he was part of something so big. The players, under enormous pressure, remained in their own cocoon most of the time, one that had them wrapped up in wool blazers that itched like the dickens, as Lindros recalls. All the players had hockey ass, which wasn't accounted for in the team-issued pants they had to wear everywhere. And it was cold. Lindros remembers it being so cold that if you went outside with wet hair, it would freeze to the point where players would pounce on unsuspecting teammates and actually break their hair. "Guys would be losing chunks of hair," he recalls. "It didn't make for the cutest team picture."

There are 22 players in that team photo, and every one of them went on to play in the NHL. Five guys played 1,000 games: Scott Niedermayer, Patrice Brisebois, Kris Draper, Brad May and Mike Sillinger, who became one of the most-travelled players in the history of the game after playing for 12 NHL teams. There are five Stanley Cup winners in Niedermayer, Draper, May, Brisebois and Martin Lapointe. And in Niedermayer, there's one of the most decorated players in the history of the game, with gold medals in every international competition imaginable, along with four Stanley Cups, a Conn Smythe Trophy, a Norris and a place in the Hall of Fame.

And then there's Lindros, whose career was interrupted and ended by injuries, a player limited to 760 games whose closest approach to the Stanley Cup came in 1997 when his Philadelphia Flyers were swept by the Detroit Red Wings in the final. Lindros is the only player on that WJC team with a Hart Trophy, and he's the only one holding the distinction of being the best player in the world for at least three years. It took seven years of eligibility before he received his call to the Hall of Fame, but it finally came in June 2016. In terms of pure power and skill, Lindros is without peer in the history of the game.

Lindros then articulates what everyone in the hockey world knows: the six concussions he suffered in less than two years were largely responsible for his premature decline as an NHL player and made him a shell of his former dominant self. The first one came March 7, 1998, when Darius Kasparaitis levelled him, and the last came 811 days later on May 26, 2000. In Game 7 of the Eastern Conference final, Scott Stevens knocked out Lindros with the kind of hit that got Stevens into the Hall of Fame but would have earned him a long suspension in today's NHL. It left Lindros curled on the ice in the fetal position. His career was never the same. "I certainly did not play as well during the latter stages of my career," Lindros says. "I hated going

through the middle. I had huge fears. It's tough going from being so assertive – you never show any cracks – to having an 'X' on your back. Players who would have never spoken or taken liberties in the past, it was happening all the time. I had a fear of cutting through the middle. Absolutely. Could I still shoot and pass? I could still score, but it wasn't the same game."

***

Here is where the redemption figures in. Lindros, along with his father, Carl, who was also his agent, criticized the Flyers' handling of his concussion issues. He was accused of getting his own doctor to handle his injury, though he says the doctor he ultimately saw, Dr. James Kelly, was recommended by the migraine specialist that the Flyers originally sent him to. Lindros' handling of his injury and his insistence on not playing until feeling healthy are the kinds of things players are encouraged

to do now. They're supposed to gather all the information they can, they're free to get their own independent opinions, and they're urged not to forsake their lives to keep playing when they shouldn't. Suddenly, Lindros doesn't look so obstinate.

It's the field of head trauma that Lindros has now immersed himself in, along with other charitable efforts. He's the honorary chair of See the Line, a concussion research and awareness effort based at Western University that assembles a symposium every summer. It was at one of those symposiums that Lindros listened to Dr. Arthur Brown, who has conducted research that points to the manipulation of white blood cells as a possible vehicle in stopping damage caused by concussions and preventing possible onset of dementia.

Lindros gets excited as he describes it. When a person receives a cut, white blood cells rush in to close the gap and form a scab so the healing can take place. When an injury occurs in the brain, though, there isn't room for that kind of expansion, which causes headaches and compression. Dr. Brown has developed a method to manipulate white blood cells so this doesn't happen and uses them to rejuvenate the nerve damage that has occurred in the stems. He has been researching this for 11 years and is at the animal testing stage, but he requires around $3.2 million to finish the human testing part.

That's where Lindros comes in. As soon as Dr. Brown finished his speech, Lindros asked how he could help. Last summer, Lindros convinced the NHL Players' Association to donate $500,000. So far, about $300,000 has come from private donations, leaving it still $2.35 million short. Lindros thinks the project could be a game-changer. "When I heard it, I was like, 'Finally, this is the first new thing I've heard in forever,' " Lindros says. "And this isn't just for athletes, it isn't just for kids playing hockey. This is for kids who fall off the jungle gym, this is for car accidents. This may spread into an area where it can even help with ALS."

Lindros does, however, lament what he thinks is a lack of cohesion in the scientific community when it comes to concussions. Instead of pooling expertise and resources, and sharing failures as well as their triumphs, Lindros sees a world in which experts are working without collaborating. "There's a bit of dysfunction there," he says. "Not everybody is playing nice in the sandbox."

Lindros is now in a place where he can concentrate on fatherhood and help with concussions in the knowledge that he did right by himself. Certainly history will paint him differently as time goes on. Some will never forgive him for not reporting to Sault Ste. Marie and Quebec. Lindros was recently at a charity hockey tournament where a Quebec native asked him to sign something and was shocked when Lindros introduced his Montreal-born wife. Lindros takes comfort in the fact that it was recently chronicled by *La Presse* that Hall of Famer Guy Lafleur, who tried to convince Lindros to come to Quebec after the Nordiques drafted him first overall in 1991, made it clear that the Lindros family's objections were with owner Marcel Aubut, not the Nordiques or the province of Quebec. "Basically, Guy was saying to Marcel Aubut, 'It's not that they have anything against French people or the city. They don't like you, Marcel,' " Lindros says.

It was an exercise in self-determination that flew in the face of old-school thinking that you go where you're told and keep your damn mouth shut. There were players both before and after Lindros who refused to play in certain NHL cities, and there are dozens of veterans in the league who now have no-trade clauses in their contracts, which allow them to determine their final destination. They're just not 18-year-old kids who haven't played a game in the NHL yet.

***

Lindros looks at his watch. After almost an hour and a half, time is winding down. He talks about the 1991 Canada Cup and how amazing it was to walk into a dressing room of future Hall of Famers in training camp, then make the team and contribute to its success as an 18-year-old. When told that if the same scenario had come up today in the World Cup of Hockey he would have had to play for Team North America (the squad of

Canadian and American players 23 and younger), Lindros is taken aback. "Is that what they're doing?" he says. "I'm so out of it. I get my news at 7 a.m. with my Shreddies, or I read CNN alerts in the tub."

As Lindros walks toward the door, he checks on the twins, who are both fast asleep. Carl Pierre clearly needs some fresh air, so one of the nannies bundles him up and places him in the stroller. A moment of peace amid all the activity. Lindros remarks on how Ryan is long and lean, while Sophie is more solid. By the time his kids enroll in university, Lindros will be approaching senior citizen status. He worries about CTE but says no-body among former players ever talks about it. He knows one of the symptoms is a short fuse, but he attributes his to the trying Toronto traffic.

Life is good for Lindros, if hectic, and all this work isn't going to complete itself. He sticks out one of his massive mitts and shakes hands with a gentleness that betrays his size and strength.

Outside, it's noticeably quiet. The man inside, however, is busy yet content, and at peace with himself. He is trying to do some good in the world, and he's looking forward to years of happiness. Good for him.

– By Ken Campbell

80 PETER STASTNY

THE MEMORY LINGERS. It never goes away. Tanks on the boulevard, soldiers in the streets.

The year was 1968. The Soviet Union had invaded Czechoslovakia and 11-year-old Peter Stastny was learning how to hate. "They were the enemy, the hated ones," Stastny said. "They were so big, and we were just a tiny speck. But in the hockey rink, it was different. We were on even terms."

In the summer of 1980, while playing in a tournament in Austria, his distaste for life behind the Iron Curtain led Stastny and brother Anton to sneak away from their Slovan Bratislava club. They defected to Canada to join the Quebec Nordiques, the first step in a process that saw all Czech and Russian players freed to join the NHL within a decade. "When we'd go to a friendship tour in West Germany, we'd get papers and read about him," said former Czech NHLer Jiri Hrdina. "Ninety percent of the people had their fingers crossed for him."

In the 1980s, Stastny put up 1,059 points – second only to Wayne Gretzky – though he scoffs at the notion that he initiated the collapse of the Iron Curtain. "There were guys ahead of me who paved the road," Stastny said. "Vaclav Nedomansky, Richard Farda, Anders Hedberg, Ulf Nilsson – they were the (European) pioneers."

Stastny is happy that the NHL is now without question where all the world's best players perform. "Players like (Russians Viacheslav) Fetisov, (Alexei) Kasatonov, they were superstars in their own country," Stastny said. "You always knew if they were given the chance to come here, they would excel."

– By Bob Duff

81 RENE LECAVALIER

ON OCT. 11, 1952, *Société Radio-Canada's* cameras delivered the first telecast of an NHL game trained on the "CH" at center ice at the Montreal Forum. Then, the first voice heard, that of Rene Lecavalier, proceeded to colorfully describe the third period of the game between the hometown Canadiens, wearing their "chandails blancs" and Detroit, in their "chandails rouges" – even though the TV picture was in black and white.

It wasn't just the start of televised hockey, but also Lecavalier's long tenure as the quintessential Francophone voice of the game. He became *La Soiree du Hockey's* top play-by-play man until the mid-1980s, bringing listeners the Canadiens' action from every Stanley Cup final and events like the 1972 Canada-Soviet Summit Series, in which his call of Paul Henderson's series-winning goal is as memorable in French-speaking Canada as Foster Hewitt's call is for English-speaking Canada.

Lecavalier's voice – calm, matter-of-fact and reassuring, until something important happened, at which point it rose to match the intensity of the play – reflected in part his background as a war correspondent. A dapper, handsome man whose grasp of culture as a whole made him a versatile announcer, he was renowned for his excellent diction and elocution.

Lecavalier's innovative use of language was most significant for hockey. Not content to employ commonly used English terms and phrases, Lecavalier found words in his native tongue, inventing the French hockey vocabulary.

He mentored others in their development as announcers, including former Canadiens winger Gilles Tremblay, the first Francophone athlete to transition to broadcasting. Many years later, countless French broadcasters afterward credited Lecavalier with being their professional inspiration.

– *By Stu Hackel*

82 VLADISLAV TRETIAK

RUSSIAN HOCKEY HAS had no greater ambassador, and no player has been held in such high respect abroad than the goalie who stunned Canada's best NHLers with his skills in the 1972 Summit Series.

North American fans were sold on Vladislav Tretiak that Saturday night in September when he acrobatically beat Canada at the Montreal Forum 7-3. Surrendering the series-winning goal to Paul Henderson in the final minute of Game 8 did little to tarnish his image.

Tretiak felt right at home in the Forum, though he never got to play for the Canadiens, who drafted him in 1983. He was spectacular in a 3-3 tie between the Habs and Central Red Army club on New Year's Eve of 1975.

Tretiak broke the hearts of Canadians but won further admiration at the Forum, performing his magic in an 8-1 rout of Canada in the final of the 1981 Canada Cup tournament. He was named the tournament MVP.

The following season, in the same hockey shrine where fans were used to worshipping the stars of the Montreal Canadiens like Maurice Richard, Jean Beliveau and Guy Lafleur, Tretiak was given a standing ovation after he shut out Les Glorieux 5-0 in front of a standing room only audience while playing for the Soviet All-Stars on New Year's Eve.

His goodwill has transcended hockey rinks. As a result of his efforts in founding Friends of Canada, an organization dedicated to fostering good relations between Canada and Russia, he became the first Russian to re-

ceive the Meritorious Service Medal from the Governor General.

Although he never played in the NHL, he was inducted into the Hall of Fame in 1989, the first non-North American-trained player to be accorded that honor.

As the only athlete competing in his fourth Olympics, Tretiak was chosen to carry the Russian flag during the Opening Ceremonies at Sarajevo in 1984. He retired after the Soviets won the gold medal in a cakewalk.

In 2006, Tretiak was elected head of the Russian Ice Hockey Federation. Russia flopped at the 2010 Olympics in Vancouver, where he served as GM, exiting in the quarterfinals following a humiliating 7-3 loss to Canada, and surprisingly bowed out again in the quarterfinals of the 2014 Olympics on home ice in Sochi. However, under his leadership, the Russian team has returned to top form in World Championship play, winning four gold medals and two silvers in the past eight years.

Tretiak was elected to the Russian State Duma in 2003 and serves as chairman of the committee on sport.

– By Denis Gibbons

83 SHELDON KENNEDY

SHELDON KENNEDY COULDN'T believe it when the news came in the winter of 2015: *Swift Current area youth hockey coach charged with sexually assaulting young boys.* It couldn't happen again, could it? Only a generation later?

If anyone is aware of the dangers of sexual predators, it's Kennedy, the former NHL right winger who stepped forward in 1996 about his years as victim of his junior coach in Swift Current, convicted pedophile Graham James. In the two decades since, Kennedy has made a second career of opening eyes and warning parents and youth associations about the dark underworld of sexual abuse.

In the midst of creating his documentary, *Swift Current*, on the trials and triumphs of Kennedy, producer Joshua Rofe told how his story's coming to light saved at least one youth, and probably many more, from falling victim to pedophiles. "A mother and son in Swift Current were watching Sheldon Kennedy receive the Order of Canada earlier last winter," Rofe recounted. "The mother said, 'Sheldon played hockey here. He was sexually abused by his coach and it took him years to step forward and tell someone. And he's been trying to spread that message ever since.' She orders Sheldon's book, continues to tell her son about Sheldon's story. Finally, the boy gathers enough courage to say, 'Mom, my coach is abusing me.'"

Shortly afterwards, police charged 39-year-old Ryan Chamberlin, a private goaltending coach working in various small towns around Swift Current, with sexual assault and child luring. Before the case proceeded to trial, more victims stepped forward. By May, Chamberlin had pled guilty in court and been sentenced to five years in prison. "We know they're out there," Kennedy said. "They're banking on you being too afraid or too ashamed to be talking about this. (Adults) have to be courageous and be a leader, otherwise you're risking the safety

of these children. We're trying to make people aware. Ask questions. Talk to your child."

The Sheldon Kennedy Child Advocacy Centre in Calgary conducts 120 investigations monthly and employs a staff of social workers, pediatricians, psychologists and psychiatrists. Kennedy's awareness group is the reason why he was awarded the Order of Canada. "This is a societal issue, not just hockey," Kennedy said. "But hockey has to be a leader in creating an awareness."

– Brian Costello

84 GLENN HALL

MAYBE IT'S HUMILITY, or perhaps he's just tired of having answered the same question for half a century. Whichever it is, Glenn Hall is matter-of-fact when talking about hockey's most untouchable record. "You had to be lucky," Hall understated. "You had to stay healthy."

Hall's record of 502 consecutive games between the pipes for Detroit and Chicago in the 1950s and '60s is an ironclad standard.

It's unusual for a skater to play that many consecutive games. For a goalie, it will never happen again. It would be a cover story in *The Hockey News* if any stopper made it to 10 percent of Hall's record. "Impossible," said noted hockey historian Ernie Fitzsimmons, from the Society of International Hockey Research. "With all the travel and the improved shooting skills by even the weakest players, and the goalie interference...that makes it impossible to go every game."

Prior to NHL's 1967 expansion, it was common for teams to rely on one goalie. In many cases, one goalie played the entire season. But Hall did it for seven consecutive years – until the morning of Nov. 7, 1962, when a pulled muscle in his back had him struggling to get out of bed. "My back started bothering me a few days before," recalled Hall, a retired rancher living in Stony Plain, Alta. "I started a (Nov. 4) game and figured the adrenaline would carry me through as it had in the past. This time, it would not."

Chicago carried a 1-0 lead into the third period of that game against Detroit, but all was not right with Hall. He allowed three goals on seven shots and the Red Wings won 3-1. Bending over to untie his skates was painful for him.

The Hawks recalled Denis DeJordy in case Hall wasn't ready for the Nov. 7 game. The streak ended at 502 games, and more than 50 years later that number is synonymous with the Hall of Fame stopper, even if it doesn't signify for Hall himself. "It's just a number," Hall said. "It doesn't mean that much. Just something that happened. Playing in the NHL was the most important thing that happened to me. That was my highlight."

At one point during his run, Hall almost walked away from the streak and the game itself. "The GM at the time (Chicago's Tommy Ivan) issued an edict that we would get a $100 fine for – what did he call it? – 'indifferent play,'" Hall said. "I got it once for not playing to my full extent. The GM said, 'If you don't like the fine, quit.' So I contemplated that. I really, really did. I went back to my wife

and we talked about it. The problem was, I didn't know how to do anything else. The only thing I knew how to do is play goalie. So I paid the ransom and continued to play. That was the closest I came to stopping the streak."

There was another close call when Hall had a reaction to a penicillin shot. He said his eyes swelled up and he could barely see through what had become two thin slits, but he recovered in time for the next game.

Hall calls the streak "lucky," but perhaps it had something to do with his notorious pre-game ritual of vomiting prior to leaving the dressing room. It was his way of psyching himself up. Hugging the porcelain seemed to work. "It was a case of playing well – I played well when I threw up before games," Hall said. "If I was just whistling relaxed, I was horses--t, so I forced myself and said, 'This is everything. You've got to play well, you've got to play well.' "

So what was the ritual, Glenn? Spoon or fingers down your throat? "No, no, no. You can do it mentally, and I'd have a glass of water and go and do it," he said. "I could do it right now if you wanted."

Take a break, Glenn. You've earned it.

– By Brian Costello

85 COLIN CAMPBELL

WHOEVER IS IN charge of NHL hockey operations has, by definition, a powerful position. That person oversees the conduct of the game, including interpretation of the rules, on-ice officials and in-game player discipline, as well as coordinating GM meetings that review those matters and set their direction.

Hall of Fame builder Brian O'Neill occupied the chair first, from 1977 until 1992, setting the parameters. But hockey changed dramatically in the 21st century, and

Colin Campbell, who took the post in 1998, stood at the center of it all.

A former rugged old-school defenseman, then a coach during the Dead Puck Era, Campbell supervised the NHL game committee and administered development camps focusing on improving entertainment value in the games. He sought feedback from various constituencies, and then, after accumulating a large amount of input, chaired the league's competition committee that established the "new rules" to open up the game after the 2004-05 lockout.

His authority to suspend or fine players for their on-ice behavior received the most attention. It is a heavy responsibility and, until he turned that function over to Brendan Shanahan in 2011, no executive in the sport sat more squarely in the crosshairs of public scrutiny and scorn.

– By Stu Hackel

86 JOHN FERGUSON SR.

SCOTTY BOWMAN REMEMBERS when John Ferguson Sr. first arrived in Montreal in 1963. "Montreal lost in the semifinals for three straight years, and they were pretty tough years," recalled Bowman, then a coach in Montreal's developmental system. "People were saying that (Canadiens coach Toe) Blake had lost it, that he didn't have the touch anymore."

Montreal developed too many players of similar skill and became undersized. "Sam Pollock took over as GM and they knew the team had to get tougher," Bowman said. "They brought in people like Ferguson, Ted Harris and Terry Harper and won four more Cups in the five years (between 1964-65 and 1968-69)."

Arriving from Cleveland of the AHL, Ferguson changed the game for the Canadiens. "You couldn't take a run at Jean Beliveau or Henri Richard or (Yvan) Cournoyer, because if you did, you had to pay the price, which was a tussle with John," former NHLer Bob Nevin recalled. Ferguson led the AHL Barons with 179 penalty minutes in 1962-63 and was second on the club with 38 goals.

He was the model tough guy, capable of playing a good, solid game but knowing when it was time to gear up and take care of business.

He struck fear into opponents.

Because scouting back then wasn't as in-depth as it is today, Nevin wasn't wary the first time he opposed Ferguson. "I'd just came to the Rangers from the Leafs, and he goes by me and gives me an elbow to the head," Nevin said. "I thought, 'Holy smokes, who's this guy?' Not knowing who he was, I actually had a fight with him over that. That was my introduction to him. When I found out who he was and what his reputation was, I thought, 'What was I thinking, picking a fight with that guy?' "

Ferguson was more than a player. As a WHA and NHL executive when most people felt Europeans were too soft to succeed in North America, he was pro-European. His Winnipeg Jets won the 1977-78 Avco Cup with eight Europeans in the lineup. "You can't win without Europeans," Ferguson said.

– By Bob Duff

87 TIM HORTON

WHEN TIM HORTON appeared on a *Hockey Night in Canada* intermission in 1968, he took the opportunity to plug his new donut business. Little did he know that he would become a household name across Canada for something other than hockey.

In 1947, the Toronto Maple Leafs added Horton to their negotiation list despite scout-

ing reports that he had poor eyesight. Obviously, the Leafs saw other qualities in him that were enough to offset this deficiency.

Nicknamed the 'Pony Express' for his frequent rushes up the ice, Horton's ability to skate was put in jeopardy in 1955 when he was involved in a devastating collision with Bill Gadsby of the New York Rangers and was stretchered off with a severely broken leg and jaw. But he would be back. Horton demonstrated his character and dedication to the game by returning midway through the following season.

His super-strength was legendary, but another one of his intangible assets was that he rarely lost his temper. The most notable time

he slipped in character was when he attacked brawny Lou Fontinato, who had jumped a teammate. However, this was only given the circumstances. Any player who played with Horton knew that he always had their backs in any altercation. He was the ultimate team man.

If the Conn Smythe Trophy was awarded in 1962, Horton would have been a sure winner, setting a playoff record for defensemen with 16 points. When paired with Allan Stanley, he was the rock on the Leafs' defense. Horton also won four Stanley Cups while garnering numerous all-star selections.

– By Paul Patskou

88 CHRIS CHELIOS

DEDICATION BUILT CHRIS Chelios' professional career, and his commitment was felt most on the United States national team.

It would have been impossible for casual viewers of the 19-year-old captain of the U.S. at the 1982 World Junior Championship to forecast Chelios' future, but not for Jim Johannson, his 1982-83 University of Wisconsin Badgers teammate. "I thought without a doubt this was going to be one of (the U.S.'s) great players," said Johannson, now senior director of USA Hockey. "He's going to help the identity and leadership of American players. And I think without a doubt he's done that, and I'm glad now I'm finding a way for him to use and exhibit that with more and more of our players and programs."

Chelios' value to USA Hockey can't be overstated. He was national team captain five times, including three Olympics, one World Cup and one world juniors. He appeared in 60 games between the junior and senior teams as the face of the program. He was inducted into the United States Hockey Hall of Fame in 2011.

None of this overshadows Chelios' NHL achievements, either. Over a 26-year career, Chelios became a Hall of Fame defenseman, racking up 185 goals and 948 points, winning three Norris Trophies and three Stanley Cups. He nearly won a fourth Norris, finishing second to Nicklas Lidstrom, when Chelios was 40 years old – an age at which most players have sailed off into the sunset. His career ended at age 48 with 1,651 games played, the fifth-most in NHL history on his retirement.

Since hanging up his skates, Chelios has worked in an advisory role with Detroit, where he spent 10 seasons of his career, and began to move up the ranks in 2015-16 when he was given an assistant coaching position. His off-ice time in Detroit has almost mirrored his USA Hockey progression.

The late stages of Chelios' playing career were a passing of the torch of the national program. Following his time there, he was around Team USA at international events such as the 2010 Olympics. He participated in training and development camps to teach the next generation. Now, Chelios appears ready to assume bigger roles with USA Hockey, like coaching, which he did at the 2016 world juniors.

When Johannson and coach Ron Wilson assembled their staff, Chelios was one of the first names considered for assistant roles. "The important thing for both of us was we knew the influence Chris could have on our players just by being himself and being around them – the competitive side that comes out of him," Johannson said.

It's that same competitive spirit that Johannson hopes Chelios can instill in the program's up-and-comers. That won't be without its challenges, though. Johannson acknowledged that Chelios is still acclimating to the scope of his influence on the young players – not an easy task for a seven-time all-star blueliner used to juggling much more.

Whether in Detroit or with USA Hockey, when players have questions, Chelios has answers. To Johannson, there's no doubt that

Chelios' dedication to improving USA Hockey is as strong as the dedication that built his 26-year career. "Knowing Chris as well as I do, I don't think that's ever going to change," Johannson said. "I say that (as a) complete compliment. If he's in something, he's all in."

– By Jared Clinton

89 JOHN COLLINS

A PARADE OF marketing executives guided the NHL's business after Don Ruck established NHL Services in the early 1970s. None ever approached John Collins' achievement of doubling annual league revenues from $2 billion to $4 billion after only nine seasons, though.

Collins' approach combined his abilities to look forward *and* backward. In 2006, he championed the NHL, joining other pro leagues in live streaming games, which proved so successful that the league was able to offload all its digital rights in 2014 to MLB Advanced Media for a reported $1.2 billion over six years.

New long-term national TV deals in Canada (with Rogers for $5.2 billion) and the U.S. (with Comcast for $2.2 billion) generated greater fiscal growth. Collins was integral to negotiating those contracts – and one element of their execution was returning the game to its roots, creating the annual outdoor Winter Classic and a revival of the Heritage Classic in Canada. The league's outdoor slate grew when it cloned the Winter Classic into various Stadium Series games.

To raise the Winter Classic's profile, Collins engaged *HBO* to develop a documentary TV series focusing on the game's two teams. The all-access show continued as a feature of future Winter Classics and some NHL clubs copied this model throughout the season, providing their fans with an unprecedented inside perspective on their team.

When confronted with the sensitive issue of jersey designs, Collins resisted the urges of his predecessors who had gifted fans with grotesque jerseys, particularly in the 1990s, to modernize hockey. He instead proved sympathetic to tradition and fans' tribal instincts by honoring the past, stressing the creation of jerseys with distinct throwback themes.

After serving as the NHL's chief operating officer since 2008, Collins announced his departure from the league in 2015.

– By Stu Hackel

90 DAVE SCHULTZ

THINK OF THE Broad Street Bullies and Dave Schultz's menacing face and flying fists usually come to mind. 'The Hammer' designed the blueprint for NHL enforcers, proving so successful in Philadelphia that the rest of the league soon followed suit, acquiring their own tough guys.

Schultz was drafted in 1969 by the Flyers. Before the 1972-73 campaign, Schultz's first NHL season, the Flyers hadn't finished above .500, nor had they won a playoff series. Schultz's arrival helped form the identity of the franchise and ushered in an era of success, despite playing only four seasons in Philly.

If the Broad Street Bully hockey is credited with the Flyers' success, then Schultz was the catalyst of the team's rock 'em sock 'em style of play. Widely recognized as the NHL's archetypal goon, Schultz recorded a league-high 259 penalty minutes in his rookie season. He followed with 348 in 1973-74, en route to the Flyers' first Stanley Cup. And the following year Schultz put up 472, a single-season record that still stands today (and is 63 more than the second on the list), on his way to back-to-back championships in Philadelphia.

Despite making their third final in 1976, the Flyers were unable to retain their crown.

That off-season, Schultz was traded to Los Angeles, and the Flyers missed him. He achieved most of his success in Philadelphia, though his reputation followed him wherever he went.

The Hammer left an impression on the game following his retirement in 1980. The Schultz Rule bans players from wearing boxing wraps under their gloves. And the enforcer template he created lasted about four decades until the league shifted toward a faster, more skilled style of play, rendering fighters endangered in today's NHL.

Schultz retired after only 535 games, leaving him 35th all-time in penalty minutes. Of players playing at least 250 games, only Chris Nilan and Shane Chulra averaged more PIMs per game than Schultz's 4.3.

– By Jacob Cohen

91 MIKE BABCOCK

PLAYERS DON'T LISTEN to Mike Babcock because he has won a Stanley Cup, two Olympic gold medals, a World Championship gold and a World Cup title. His talents as a communicator, teacher and motivator – none of which waver when circumstances are unfavorable – are why he can coach a team to a championship (as he did for the 2007-08 Detroit Red Wings) as easily as he can keep a last-place squad to believe its best days are ahead (as he did for the 2015-16 Toronto Maple Leafs). "Nothing changes, which in itself is impressive," said Leafs defenseman Morgan Rielly. "Each day he approaches the game with the same enthusiasm and attitude, and I really think that goes a long way. He's one of the hardest workers I've seen, and the players really feed off that."

In an era when NHL coaches have a limited shelf life, Babcock survived a decade in Detroit before leaving for Toronto. He's widely regarded as the best coach of his generation, as evidenced by the record-setting eight-year, $50-million contract he signed with the Maple Leafs in the summer of 2015.

– By Adam Proteau

92 ANGELA JAMES

LOOK OUT, HOCKEY world: Angela James is making a comeback. At the age of 52 and after missing three years with an injury, perhaps not too much should be expected, even in a women's beer league that plays at an ungodly hour. Then again, with James, you never know.

There were women who made their names in hockey before James, but it would be difficult to find one who had a more profound effect on the game. The captain of Canada's first women's World Championship team in 1990 was a trailblazer in every sense of the word when it came to opening avenues for women to play this game. James has often been referred to as "the Wayne Gretzky of women's hockey," but in reality she's more like a female version of Howie Morenz, who was the first true superstar ever to play in the NHL.

The fact that James even has a women's beer league to play in at an ungodly hour is, in part, a testament to her impact on the game. And when she watches from the bench while her 10-year-old daughter Toni plays house league hockey, sometimes she contemplates her place in all of that. Not often, but sometimes. "I couldn't even take that credit, because there were girls before me that I used to go down to the rink and watch play," James said. "I just loved the game. I look now and I'm so happy that girls are able to do that now, too."

James' hockey exploits have landed her in five Halls of Fame: the Hockey Hall of Fame, the IIHF Hall of Fame, Canada's Sports Hall of Fame, Black Hockey and Sports Hall of Fame

and the Seneca College Hall of Fame. The arena in inner city Toronto where she started out playing organized hockey at the age of eight also bears her name. It was at that arena that James started her hockey journey before jumping into girls' hockey two years later. But not only did James carve a path as one of the greatest women players ever to play the game, she did so under the most modest of circumstances. The child of a white Canadian woman and a black man who fled Mississippi to escape racial segregation, James grew up in an Ontario housing project where there was an outdoor rink. That was where James found her escape, as well as a place where she could hone her skills against the boys, including Jamal Mayers, who is the godson of James' mother. "Back then, they shoved me in net, of course, right? Because you're a girl," James said. "So then I decided to get my own equipment. I don't even know how I got the equipment – I probably stole it – but then I got to play out. That's how it kind of worked back then."

James and her mother experienced pushback when she tried to play with the boys in organized hockey, which she did for two years before moving over to the girls' game full time. "My mom knew every night I was down at the outdoor rink, and it wasn't until one of the neighbors said to her, 'You know, Angela is quite a good hockey player,' that I started really playing," James said. "Not long after that, Justine Blainey kind of challenged the whole system (by legally winning the right to play in a boys' league), but we wer-

en't very political and I had already moved over to girls' hockey. I really didn't have too much control at that time of my own destiny."

Hockey, however, gave her that control. It forced her to focus on the game and her studies and landed her at Seneca College in Toronto, where she was a superstar in both hockey and softball. One year at Seneca she scored 50 goals and 73 points in 14 games. Not only was her No. 8 retired by the school, she remains there as its senior sports coordinator.

James went on to play in three more women's World Championships and was the controversial last cut from the 1998 Olympic team when women's hockey made its Olympic Games debut. Despite that, James continued to play at the highest level of women's hockey and was named MVP of the Canadian Women's League six times. After retiring from competitive play, she turned to refereeing and coaching. Not only does she coach her daughter's team, she also helps coach her son Christian's midget AA team. It has been an odyssey filled with struggles and triumphs, one that has landed James in a place where she never thought she would be. It has brought her more fame and opportunities than she ever thought possible. "I don't think anybody would have thought back then that all of this would have happened," James said. "Nobody would have ever thought we'd be recognized just for playing a game that we love. Sometimes I have to think about it and say, 'Did that really happen?'"

– By Ken Campbell

93 KEN HOLLAND

IF NOT FOR the intervention of a hockey lifer by the name of Bill Dineen, Ken Holland might have become the best damn vacuum cleaner salesman Vernon, B.C. has ever seen. Alas, the owners of high-pile carpets in the heart of the picturesque Okanagan Valley never did get to experience Holland's unique charm, but the hockey world is better off for it.

First, the backstory. It was the summer of 1985, and after nine years of bouncing around as a minor league goalie with a career save percentage in the .800s, Holland had been told by the Detroit Red Wings his contract wouldn't be renewed. He was working at the liquor store in Vernon, and his wife, Cindi, was a nurse at the hospital. They had had three of their four children, and it was time to think about life after hockey. The plan was for Cindi to work and for Ken to go to school, first to Okanagan College in Vernon, then to the University of British Columbia. All he knew at that time was he really liked working with numbers, and he had a knack for organizing things.

One day, when he came home from work at the liquor store, his mother candidly asked him what his life plan was, so he told her what he and Cindi had going: He was going to work at the liquor store until Labour Day weekend, then go off to college to do something with numbers. "She said, 'Ken, you're 29 years old, and you're the man of the family, you're the breadwinner in the family. You have to put the food on the table,'" Holland recalled. "And I said, 'Mom, I have a Grade 12 education, and I played nine years of pro hockey. That's all I know.' "

That's when his mother not-so-subtly informed him the *Vernon News* was carrying an advertisement looking for an Electrolux vacuum cleaner salesman. She even went so far as to call the number and found out the job was still open. For every vacuum cleaner he sold, he would get 40 percent of the profit. She told him she'd be his first customer, and Grandma Geisbrecht, her mother, would be his second. "I thought, 'Boy, this isn't a bad gig,'" Holland said. "So I asked her, 'Any idea of the status of

Aunt Eva's vacuum cleaner?' because Aunt Eva lived two doors down from Grandma Geisbrecht. For a brief second there, I thought I was going to be a vacuum cleaner salesman."

That's where Dineen came in. He'd coached Holland with the Red Wings farm team in Adirondack the two previous seasons, and he often got a ride with Dineen to the rink for road trips. Dineen liked Holland and suggested to Red Wings GM Jim Devellano that he hire Holland as a western Canada scout. Two days after the vacuum cleaner conversation, he was interviewed over the phone by Devellano and scout Neil Smith and landed the job.

Since then, Holland has been one of the most independent, innovative and for-

ward-thinking people in the game – perhaps in its history – along with the likes of Art Ross, Scotty Bowman and Lester Patrick. And he takes his responsibility as a caretaker of the game every bit as seriously as they did.

After five years of lobbying and calling every GM individually before the GM meetings, he finally managed to spearhead the move to 3-on-3 overtime, an innovation that no less an authority than Wayne Gretzky said was "one of the best things we've done in hockey in the last 20 years." It reduced the number of games ending in shootouts to just 8.7 percent in the 2015-16 season. More importantly, however, it has injected an enormous dose of excitement and unpredictability into what used to be a defensive chess game followed by a goaltending competition.

But that's hardly at the top of the list of Holland's accomplishments. His team has won three Stanley Cups with him as GM and qualified for the post-season each year for a quarter century unitl 2017. And he has spawned a league of copycats. You know all those rookie tournaments NHL teams have now before training camp? That was Holland's idea, and the Red Wings run the best rookie tournament in the league out of Traverse City, Mich. Notice how everybody these days has four lines that can score? Well, the Red Wings have been doing that since Connor McDavid was in diapers. Puck pressure tactics instead of playing the trap? Red Wings again. Front-loaded contracts? Yup, Red Wings. Keeping your prospects in the AHL instead of rushing them into the NHL? Detroit again.

The Red Wings were putting the focus on drafting and developing players long before it became fashionable and even longer before it became necessary because of the salary cap. "You ask me if I have ideas," Holland said. "I have lots of ideas, and I have lots of ideas. Some of them are great ideas that work, and some of them didn't work out quite as well."

The ideas come because Holland's mind is always active, always constructing and deconstructing. Dallas Stars GM Jim Nill, a former teammate in junior and executive protégé, saw it for years when he was with the Red Wings as Holland's assistant GM. An office conversation about hockey would start between him and Holland, then Steve Yzerman would drift in followed by Ryan Martin, and it would continue through lunch. Or they'd go on the road to see a draft prospect and stop for something to eat. "Next thing you know, we've got out the napkins and we're doing our draft list," Nill said. "It would be, 'OK, let's do the top 10,' then, 'Let's do the top 15,' and away we would go. He has a great mind, and he can really think on his feet."

Holland has more in store for the hockey world. He's always thinking about ways to improve the game but doesn't want to share them publicly only to hear them debated by talking heads before the GMs have even had time to digest them. Some of them will be brilliant, as 3-on-3 was. Others not so much, like the executive compensation scheme, a plan that was killed after only one year by the board of governors. But Holland will keep them coming.

So he's not exactly King Midas, but he's well above the Mendoza line when it comes to successful outcomes, both for his team and for the game. Holland has a few things rattling around in his head, and they'll need to come out some day. And there will be more after that. When you're on a roll the way Holland is, you just keep thinking.

– By Ken Campbell

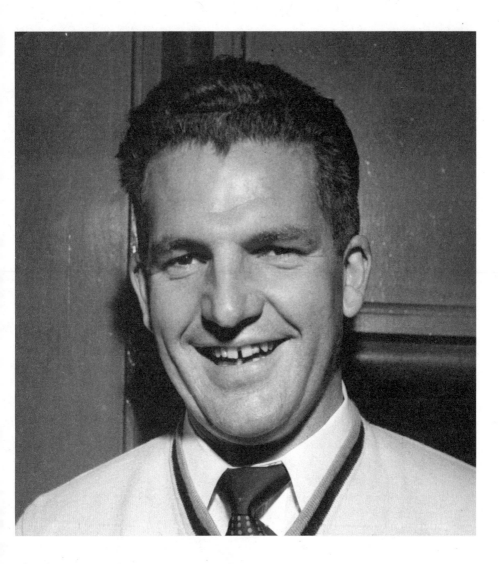

94 BILL CHADWICK

BILL CHADWICK CHANGED the way referees call a hockey game. The Manhattan, N.Y., native would have been remembered only as the league's first American-born official had it not been for a fateful night during the Stanley Cup playoffs when a raucous crowd made it virtually impossible for Chadwick to verbalize his penalty calls. "There was so much noise that I had difficulty communicating with the penalty timekeeper," Chadwick told writer John Halligan. "So I began using a kind of sign language."

Chadwick's solution to the problem was to develop a series of hand signals to represent infractions. He tapped his elbow for elbowing, chopped his hand across his arm for slashing and behind his knee to indicate tripping. The hands-on referee admitted that he couldn't specifically recollect the exact year he introduced this innovation, other than that it was during the Second World War. The NHL didn't officially adopt his series of hand signals until 1956.

Amazingly, Chadwick worked nearly 1,000 NHL games despite being legally blind in his right eye. His eye was damaged when hit with a puck in 1935, and two years later, after a minor injury to his left eye, he opted to give up playing hockey and turned to officiating. "My condition didn't hamper me," Chadwick told Stan Fischler in *Those Were the Days: The Lore of Hockey*. "I had 20/20 vision in my good left eye and was on top of the play even more than they are now. I was never away from the net when there was a play on goal."

By 1939, he was an NHL linesman at the age of 24 and moved up to referee a year later, handling the whistle until 1955.

Chadwick would get a chuckle, though, out of occasions when players or fans suggested he was blind. "I knew they were half right," Chadwick said.

– By Bob Duff

 MIKE ILITCH

AROUND THE TIME the late Mike Ilitch opened his first Little Caesars pizza restaurant in 1959, the Detroit Red Wings were in the initial stages of a decline that turned into what fans of the once-powerful franchise termed 'The Dead Wings Era.'

In 1982, with the Wings languishing at the bottom of the NHL, pizza baron Ilitch swooped in and purchased the team for $8 million from Bruce Norris, whose father bought the Detroit club in 1932. Turning around this moribund franchise required no quick fix.

Initially, Ilitch threw money at the problem, signing plenty of free agents and undrafted college players, but it wasn't until 1987 that Detroit finally won a playoff series. "Those years could have been very frustrating," said Ilitch, who passed away in February

2017 at the age of 87. "I was confused for a while, but I learned to look at hockey as a business."

He discovered money alone couldn't buy a championship. "I want to win," Ilitch said. "But you've got to have management and all the rest. It's not always a matter of spending money."

Eventually, by hiring solid management, patiently building from within and then surrounding the core with free agent acquisitions, the Wings became the most successful franchise in the NHL. They've won four Stanley Cups in the past 20 years and made the playoffs for 25 successive seasons until 2017.

As much as he wants to view his team as a business, Ilitch admitted the fan inside him often rules the day. "Sometimes I think the fan part of me takes over and it hurts (my objectivity) a little," Ilitch said. "I'm a little impulsive, but I've been in franchise sports for a while now, so I'll be OK."

In 2015, *Forbes* estimated the Wings franchise was worth $600 million. The empire will only grow when the new $650 million Detroit Events Center opens as the team's new home in 2017.

– By Bob Duff

96 TOMMY GORMAN

THOSE CLOSE TO him knew Tommy Gorman simply as 'T.P.' or 'TayPay.' Those familiar with his work knew him as the P.T. Barnum of hockey.

There was little within the structure of a hockey team that Gorman couldn't handle, but perhaps his greatest asset was his indefatigable ability to promote the sport.

A former newspaperman, Gorman was aware of the value of currying favor with editors. "He was an exciting writer, even if he wasn't accurate," said former NHLer Frank Boucher.

Gorman always spun a yarn that would fill papers. Whether he was waxing eloquent about his own team or launching a scandalous tale about the opposition, it was always a story that was sure to sell tickets. His feuds with Canadiens owner Leo Dandurand and Boston GM Art Ross were legendary. "There was a time when I denounced him at least once a day," Gorman said of Ross.

He was always thinking big picture. "It never pays to look back or worry about yesterday," Gorman told the *Ottawa Citizen*.

During his NHL career, Gorman was coach or GM of seven Stanley Cup winners. He is credited with being one of the creators of early forechecking systems. An article in the 1934 *Nashua Telegraph* wrote that Gorman's Black Hawks won the Stanley Cup that year as a result of the newly invented forecheck, which he implemented in the last six weeks of the season.

He was there, representing the Ottawa Senators, when the NHL was formed in 1917. He helped launch hockey in the Big Apple with the 1925-26 New York Americans. Gorman was the first man to coach separate teams to consecutive Stanley Cups: the 1933-34 Chicago Black Hawks and the 1934-35 Montreal Maroons. Later, he managed the Montreal Canadiens to two Stanley Cup titles.

His players absolutely loved him. "They can say what they like about Gorman, but he's good with the players," Canadiens forward Murph Chamberlain told the *Montreal Gazette*. "He gets the money for us."

– *By Bob Duff*

97 MANON RHEAUME

MANON RHEAUME'S STINTS at a couple Tampa Bay Lightning training camps resulted in the phrase "publicity stunt" being thrown around more times than Wayne Gretzky scored goals. To the generation of female players that followed, however, she became the face of women's hockey, securing her place among the likes of Billie Jean King.

In 1992, Rheaume became the first female to play in one of North America's four major pro sports leagues, stopping seven of nine shots in a pre-season game for the expansion Lightning against the St. Louis Blues. Not only did she go on to play for a handful of minor league teams, Rheaume blazed the trail for the likes of Hayley Wickenheiser, Angela Ruggiero and Shannon Szabados to play in men's pro leagues.

– *By Randy Sportak*

98 THE MCMURTRY BROTHERS ——

AS THE RISE in on-ice violence began gripping pro hockey in the early 1970s, roughhousing incidents filtered down to the youth leagues. After a bloody start to an Ontario Jr. B championship series in 1974 caused the Bramalea Blues to withdraw after one game, the provincial government ordered an inquiry.

Toronto attorney William McMurtry, who had played collegiately and recreationally afterward, conducted hearings in which he even got testimony from Bobby Hull and NHL president Clarence Campbell and produced a heavily researched report.

In his "Investigation and Inquiry into Violence in Amateur Hockey," McMurtry laid blame squarely on the pro game, which he said kids emulate, and called for tougher fighting penalties in the NHL to change the game's culture.

His report set off a months-long debate, a public firestorm of charges and counter-charges raging in the media on both sides of the border. But Campbell had no intention of making changes, maintaining that fighting was a necessary "safety valve" and that society accepted the game's violence.

Following a year of inaction by the pros, in October 1975, McMurtry's brother, Roy, Ontario's new attorney general, directed police and prosecutors to treat egregious incidents during games as if they had occurred on the street.

The NHL continued to maintain that it should police its game itself, but in November the Crown charged Detroit's Dan Maloney with assault after he attacked Brian Glennie,

an unsuspecting Toronto player, at Maple Leaf Gardens. Maloney eventually pled no contest, accepting a sentence of community service and a two-year ban from playing in Toronto.

But that triggered at least four other prosecutions over the next two years in which violent on-ice episodes at various levels of hockey ended in court around North America, including another brought by McMurtry against four members of the Flyers for brawling during a playoff game in Toronto.

Not every jurisdiction brought charges against players for violent behavior during games, but as the trials of Marty McSorley and Todd Bertuzzi in the 21st century demonstrated, the McMurtry brothers' thinking left a mark on prosecutors.

– By Stu Hackel

WILLIAM MCMURTRY

ROY MCMURTRY (LEFT) WITH TORONTO MAPLE LEAFS' DICK DUFF

99 STAN FISCHLER

BEFORE BLOGS, TWITTER and the NHL Network – before there was much TV coverage, in fact – there was Stan Fischler, someone hockey fans have turned to for more than six decades for an inside look at the game and its personalities.

Fischler, now 85, earned his moniker as 'The Hockey Maven' over a long career as a well-sourced hockey writer turned broadcaster. Fresh out of college, he landed a job with the New York Rangers that led to a newspaper gig. That led to assignments from national publications and evolved into his current role as a TV analyst. "I was networking," Fischler said, "not even knowing what networking was."

Hitting his stride as expansion arrived in the 1960s, Fischler introduced a generation of baby boomers to NHL life through books such as *Bobby Orr and the Big, Bad Bruins.*

Fischler estimates that he and his late wife, Shirley, have written about 100 books, including those about his other passion, subway systems. He points to one of their books as groundbreaking: *The Hockey Encyclopedia,* first published in 1975. "It was mostly her work," Fischler said. "And it was a very tough thing to do because the NHL was primitive in the way it handled statistics."

Number crunchers, tip your hats.

– By David Pollak

100 MIKE EMRICK

ON A CRISP October morning in Philadelphia, Mike 'Doc' Emrick strides through the hallways of Wells Fargo Center. Wearing a Bowling Green State University polo shirt, a nod to his alma mater where he earned his PhD in radio-television-film (hence the nickname) and an NBC Olympics windbreaker, he's all smiles. He has broadcasted more than 3,000 professional hockey games, but to him the most important is always the one he's about to call.

It's 10:30 a.m., but Emrick woke up early, taking the train from Connecticut where he and his wife of nearly four decades have been visiting family. Hockey is his passion, but his life always has and always will revolve around his wife, Joyce, their menagerie of two dogs and five horses and the many trips they take together throughout each year. But for the entirety of this morning's nearly five-hour train ride, his focus was on his work. As NBC's lead hockey play-by-play broadcaster, he has perused dozens of pages of game notes, statistics, historical facts and stories, just as he does every day in preparation for calling a game. Today, it's Blackhawks versus Flyers.

As Emrick, 70, walks at ice level toward an empty dressing room to unpack his belongings, he's swarmed by dozens of people. Some are old friends, players, coaches and fellow media members, while others are trying to meet him for the first time. He appears genuinely happy to see each of them and spends as much time with them as possible before he has to excuse himself for the morning skate. Preparation for tonight's game beckons.

Emrick, the acknowledged national TV voice of the NHL and Olympic hockey in the United States for decades, exerts his influence in ways so subtle even he is unaware of them. While many others look to actively affect the game, Emrick's influence seems to disperse by osmosis. For Doc, it is never about himself but rather those he passes in the hallways of NHL arenas with whom few would think to strike up a conversation. He sees someone for the first time in years and remembers to ask how their kid is doing. He makes those around him feel as if they're the ones whose voices will be heard by millions each night. His respect for the value of each is genuine, irrespective of how humble or grand they may be.

For a man so well-known in the hockey world, Emrick seems shocked at the admiration he garners. After the morning skate, he runs into four members of the 2014 United States Olympic women's hockey team, in town for a charity event. As honored as they are to meet the man who made their names known throughout the U.S., he appears just as humbled to meet them. While chatting casually with them, the smile on his face mirrors that of a child meeting his hero.

Minutes later, Emrick spots an 11-year-old boy in a heavily autographed Blackhawks jersey standing with his dad in the hallway. After chatting with him for a few minutes, Emrick discovers that the young fan spent the summer creating his own list

of the top 100 all-time NHL players and wanted to share it. Emrick's eyes light up. He sits in the hallway beside his newest friend, debating the rankings: Bill Mosienko versus Bill Cowley, Frank McGee versus Sprague Cleghorn, Mario Lemieux versus Jaromir Jagr and more. After a lengthy conversation in which Emrick seemed to learn more than the young fan, he tells the kid's father, "I want a photocopy of that," and walks back to the stands.

Emrick shares the young fan's studiousness. At 70, he remains a student of the game. He has binders filled with information on every player: statistics, trends, historical facts and stories he's kept in his pocket for years until just the right moment.

Above all else, Emrick is a pure fan. He's enthusiastic about those players who toiled in the minors before making it to the NHL. While other media members surround the superstars prior to the game, Emrick quietly talks with rookies and others who worked their way up from the minor leagues. Each night it gives him not only fodder for the broadcast, but also personal satisfaction.

As the game nears, Emrick appears in the broadcast booth at 6 p.m. a completely different man. Gone is his playful smile and casual personality. Suited up for the pregame taping, he now radiates an aura of focus and intensity. His expression indicates the importance of this night. Every broadcast is an opportunity to win a new fan for the sport he loves most, creating a chance to make a lasting impression on someone tuning in to a hockey game for the first time. He strives for perfection each time and takes his job in the booth as seriously as every player on the ice.

The NBC booth looks chaotic during the game, but Emrick articulates the action with artistry. He performs with precision and accuracy, rarely looking at his cheat sheet, as if he has memorized all those pages of notes in merely a few hours. In the second period, after a series of exciting back-and-forth plays, he leans back in his chair smirking, turns to fellow game analyst Eddie Olczyk and chimes on-air, "Isn't this great?"

The influence Emrick has exerted on hockey is immeasurable, if only because of its subtlety. Whether meeting him on the street, spotting him in the arena or simply hearing him on a broadcast, fans are drawn to Emrick's warm personality and his genuine love for what he does. While many well-known people seem burdened by professional obligations that cut into personal time, Emrick clearly treasures them. He dives wholeheartedly into meeting someone new, reacquainting himself with an old friend and even making a child's day. His generosity and passion transfer to those around this master communicator of the game who can't help but be in a giving mood after a chat with this truly "good doctor" of hockey.

As the final buzzer sounds, he signs off after another broadcast. Almost as quickly as he came, he bolts out of the booth with a smile and a wink. Tomorrow, he'll again begin preparing for the most important game of his career.

– By Alan Bass

ACKNOWLEDGMENTS

MANY THANKS ARE due for what was truly a team effort:

The Hockey News' management team – Jason Kay, editor in chief; and Edward Fraser, managing editor – for their work behind the scenes.

Leanne Gilbert, for her vision and design, and Shea Berencsi, for tracking down every photo.

Colin Elliott, Silvana Sciortino and Angela Valentini, THN's marketing and communications team, for getting the word out across the hockey world.

THN staffers Ken Campbell, Jared Clinton, Brian Costello, Ian Denomme, Ryan Kennedy and Matt Larkin, for weaving some wicked yarns.

Freelance writers Shelly Anderson, Mike Brophy, Rich Chere, Bob Duff, Stan Fischler, Wayne Fish, Denis Gibbons, Stu Hackel, Pat Hickey, Casey Ippolito, Brian McNally, Paul Patskou, David Pollak, Adam Proteau, George Richards and Eric Zweig, for their expertise and coverage.

The book's 10 expert panelists Alan Adams, Ken Campbell, Steve Dryden, Bob Duff, Helene Elliott, Kerry Fraser, Stu Hackel, Pierre McGuire, Paul Patskou and Szymon Szemberg.

Fearless fact-checker Malcolm Campbell, for exorcizing all of the devils hiding in the dirty details.

Rachel Villari, for her careful copy editing, and Luke Sawczak, for his attentive proofreading.

THN's cadre of intrepid interns, Chris Ciligot, Jacob Cohen, Matthew Cranker, Nicole Dawe, Alex Debets, Chris Jones, Emma Mason, Michael Fletcher, Jimmy Huynh, Isabella Krzykala, Taylor Retter and Matthew Stamper, for all of their hard work from beginning to end.

And especially Jessica Ross, for her steady hand throughout the entire process.

PHOTO CREDITS

1   Bruce Bennett/Getty Images (2)
2   Minas Panagiotakis/Getty Images
3   HHOF Images
4   Focus On Sport/Getty Images;
    Denis Brodeur/Getty Images
5   Dave Sandford/Getty Images/NHLI
6   Bruce Bennett/Getty Images
7   Bruce Bennett/Getty Images
8   Tom Pidgeon/Getty Images
9   Pictorial Parade/Getty Images
10 Pictorial Parade/Getty Images
11 Harold Barkley/Toronto Star via
    Getty Images
12 Melchior DiGiacomo/Getty Images
13 Bruce Bennett/Getty Images
14 HHOF Images
15 Bruch Bennett/Getty Images
16 Denis Brodeur/NHLI/
    via Getty Images
17 Adam D'Oliveira Photography
18 Bruch Bennett/Getty Images
19 Bruce Bennett/Getty Images
20 Doug Griffin/Toronto Star via
    Getty Images
21 Bruch Bennett/Getty Images
22 Bruch Bennett/Getty Images
23 FPG/Getty Images
24 Bruce Bennett/Getty Images
25 Bruce Bennett/Getty Images
26 Bernard Weil/Toronto Star via
    Getty Images
27 HHOF Images
28 HHOF Images
29 Bruce Bennett/Getty Images
30 Hockey Hall of Fame
31 HHOF Images
32 HHOF Images
33 Pictorial Parade/Getty Images
34 Bruch Bennett/Getty Images
35 Bruch Bennett/Getty Images
36 Bruch Bennett/Getty Images
37 Bruce Bennett/Getty Images
38 Bruce Bennett/Getty Images

39 Hartland: HHOF Images;
    Geoff: Montreal Canadiens
40 Hockey Hall of Fame
41 Hockey Hall of Fame
42 Melchior DiGiacomo/Getty Images
43 Bruce Bennett/Getty Images
44 Courtesy of Ralph Mellanby
45 Graig Abel/NHLI via Getty Images
46 Bruce Bennett/Getty Images
47 HHOF Images
48 George Rose/Getty Images
49 Aaron Bell/OHL Images
50 Don Dutton/Toronto Star via
    Getty Images
51 Bruce Bennett/Getty Images
52 Bruce Bennett/Getty Images
53 Steve Babineau/NHLI via
    Getty Images
54 Dave Sandford/NHLI via
    Getty Images
55 Bruce Bennett/Getty Images
56 Frank Lennon/Toronto Star via
    Getty Images
57 Bruce Bennett/Getty Images
58 Bruce Bennett/Getty Images;
    Steve Babineau/NHLI via
    Getty Images
59 B. Bettencourt/Toronto Star via
    Getty Images
60 Rick Madonik/Toronto Star via
    Getty Images
61 Len Lahman/Los Angeles Times via
    Getty Images
62 Dick Loek/Toronto Star via
    Getty Images
63 Melchior DiGiacomo/Getty Images
64 Mitchell Layton/Getty Images;
    Linda Cataffo/NY Daily News
    Archive via Getty Images
65 Abelimages/Getty Images
66 Bruce Bennett/Getty Images
67 Bruce Bennett/Getty Images
68 Bruch Bennett/Getty Images
69 Bob Riha Jr/WireImage

70 Elsa/Getty Images;
    Jim McIsaac/Stringer
71 HHOF Images
72 Dave Sandford/NHLI via
    Getty Images; Patrick Smith/
    Getty Images
73 Bruce Bennett/Getty Images
74 Dave Sandford/NHLI via
    Getty Images
75 Jim McIsaac/Getty Images
76 Hockey Hall of Fame
77 Robert Laberge/ALLSPORT
78 Bruce Bennett/Getty Images
79 Denis Brodeur/NHLI via
    Getty Images; Bruce Bennett/
    Getty Images
80 Scott Levy/Getty Images
81 Hockey Hall of Fame
82 Bruch Bennett/Getty Images
83 Bill Clark/CQ Roll Call
84 Tony Triolo /Sports Illustrated/
    Getty Images
85 Bruce Bennett/Getty Images
    for NHLI
86 HHOF Images
87 Bruce Bennett/Getty Images
88 Bruch Bennett/Getty Images
89 Bruce Bennett/Getty Images
90 Bruce Bennett/Getty Images
91 Martin Rose/Getty Images
92 Seneca College in Toronto/MCT via
    Getty Images
93 Dave Reginek/NHLI via
    Getty Images
94 HHOF Images
95 Robert Laberge/Allsport
96 HHOF Images
97 Bruch Bennett/Getty Images
98 Roy: Doug Griffin/Toronto Star via
    Getty Images; William: Dick Darrell/
    Toronto Star via Getty Images
99 Jonathan Fickies/Getty Images
100 NBC Sports Group